MW00573352

HEAL OR

REPEAT:

Breaking The Cycle Of

Intergenerational Trauma

To Tee, I Love you & I hope you enjoy!

By: Jared Washington, MA, LPC

Copyright © 2020 by H.O.P.E. LLC

ISBN: 978-1-7361688-5-1

All rights reserved. No part of this publication may be reproduced, distributed, or transmitted in any form or by any means, including photocopying, recording, or other electronic or mechanical methods, without the prior written permission of the publisher, except in the case of brief quotations embodied in critical reviews and certain other noncommercial uses permitted by copyright law.

Under no circumstances will any blame or legal responsibility be held against the publisher, or author, for any damages, reparation, or monetary loss due to the information contained within this book, either directly or indirectly.

LEGAL NOTICE:

This book is copyright protected. It is only for personal use. You cannot amend, distribute, sell, use, quote, or paraphrase any part, or the content within this book, without the consent of the author or publisher.

DISCLAIMER NOTICE:

Please note the information contained within this document is for educational and entertainment purposes only. All effort has been executed to present accurate, up-to-date, reliable, complete information. No warranties of any kind are declared or implied. Readers acknowledge that the author is not engaged in the rendering of legal, financial, medical, or professional advice. The content within this book has been derived from various sources. Please consult a licensed professional before attempting any techniques outlined in this book.

By reading this document, the reader agrees that under no circumstances is the author responsible for any losses, direct or indirect, that are incurred as a result of the use of the information contained within this document, including, but not limited to, errors, omissions, or inaccuracies.

For permission requests, write to the publisher, addressed,

"Attention: Permissions Coordinator," at the address below.

H.O.P.E LLC

Atlanta, GA.

Published in the United States of America

DEDICATION

First, I would like to thank God for making all of this possible. This book is dedicated to my Family and Friends who had a hand in the creation and development of this book. Furthermore, this book is dedicated to the ancestors that came before me and paved the way as well as the Black community.

CONTENTS

CHAPTER THREE: What is Intergenerational Trauma? 43

CHAPTER FOUR: The Generational Transmission of Trauma 54

INTRODUCTION

The longer we live, the more certain it is that we will experience trauma. Trauma is the reaction to a deeply distressing or disturbing occurrence that upsets an individual's ability to cope, causes feelings of helplessness, reduces their sense of self and their ability to perceive the full range of emotions and experiences. It does not discriminate, and it exists throughout the world. We all face a traumatic experience at some points, although it may be at different levels, and the way we handle them varies.

I recently read a story of an African American girl called Jane (not her real name). For the foremost two decades of her life, you can say that she has been in child welfare for like half of the years. Since the beginning of high school and her youth advocacy journey, she has dealt with a handful of problems. Most of these issues were repercussions and difficulties that sprang up from intergenerational trauma in her family. Her mother struggled with the use of drugs throughout this period. However, she hit rock bottom when Jane and her brother decided it was safer for them to be elsewhere than in their mother's care. According to Jane, "In my times of need, when I needed my mother the most, she was not available, as she was the one

1

causing the hurt I was experiencing in the first place." Her heart broke every time she learned she wasn't home. Being the eldest daughter and sister, the household care weighed down on her shoulders; the "motherly" and parental role in the household.

In Grade 12, in between winter and spring, help was not forthcoming. As African Americans, they were expected to fend for themselves and do some jobs to help with their upkeep. Therefore, together with her brother, they called Child and Family Services, asking for help. That moment that led up to their ultimate decision was heartbreaking but undeniably courageous. Old wounds were revealed, and they had little or no understanding of what was going to happen. 'Were they going to be abused again, like when they were younger? What were they going to have to do to survive as expected of a Black child? Would it be the same as their other childhood experiences?' Those were the thoughts that keep recurring in their minds as they awaited help from the Child and Family Services.

They were afraid, but that turned into hope rather quickly. The support they received in care granted them security; their needs were met, and the heavyweight, especially on her, was lifted off her shoulders. It was a breath of fresh air after enduring the worst times of her life. However, pushing through dark and hurtful times and learning about myself had been a great ordeal. Whenever she needed guidance, she still found herself resulting in tobacco. This occurrence has been a big struggle for her.

Although healing had already commenced, not only for herself but also for her immediate family, her understanding that healing is always happening resonates a great deal of happiness, which her spirit rejoices to. She knows that she has the willpower to change within her family and be the person she needed growing up. Like she heard from her mother, "You will be the one to break the cycle." As much as her mother attempted during her younger years, she was unsuccessful in breaking the cycle, but she never gave up hope. So also, Jane is determined not to give up.

Trauma is naturally understood as a person's reaction to a major catastrophic event that is so devastating, it leaves that individual unable to come to terms with it. A traumatized person can sense a range of emotions as soon as the event is over and in the long term. They may feel upset, helpless, shocked, or have difficulty processing their experiences. Trauma can also cause physical symptoms and can have long-term effects on a person's well-being. If symptoms persist and do not reduce in severity, it can indicate that the trauma has developed into a mental health disorder referred to as post-traumatic stress disorder (PTSD).

In some cases, trauma is passed down from the first generation of survivors who directly experienced or witnessed traumatic events to future generations. This case is referred to as intergenerational trauma and can be passed on through parenting practices, behavioral problems, violence, harmful substance use, and mental health issues. Intergenerational trauma has been seen as experienced in Blacks in the United States of America.

Intergenerational trauma is stress-induced trauma that's transferred from one generation to the next when left untreated. In Indigenous contexts, it's common among children of survivors of Black People residing in America and their communities. No family or individual is exempt from traumatic encounters that can lastingly affect the individual just like their relatives. When contemplating trauma and its effect, numerous individuals consider war veterans. In any case, 60% of men and half of the women are involved with at least one horrible mishap during their lifetime (U. S. Division of Veteran Undertakings, 2020). These traumatic mishaps can be, however, not restricted to rough handling (physical, sexual, enthusiastic), deaths, accidents, war, and different chaos. The effect of trauma can influence the person as much as the generations yet unborn. To the casualties of memorable trauma, this injury was so problematic to their lifestyle before the attack (involving the continued staggering impacts of such terrible sustained cycles) that its resultant effects are as yet still felt now by their descendants. This is the reason it's essential to comprehend this idea, tune in to their accounts and understand that their continuous agony can't be forgotten about as "It's an ideal opportunity to proceed onward as of now." It is so significant for approaches and changes to be set up with Black People in America at the cutting edge to cure the ages of trauma.

This book, Heal or Repeat: Breaking the Cycle of Intergenerational Trauma, reveals the basis of intergenerational trauma, what it is, its history, the history of slavery in America, how it all began, how trauma is transmitted from one generation to another, and some historical events of traumatic racial events that are still interconnected to the happenings of this day. Most importantly, Heal or Repeat: Breaking the Cycle of Intergenerational Trauma reveals the impact of intergenerational trauma on Black people in America, how to begin healing, how the chain of this cycle can be broken; and not further passed on to the next generation.

Therefore, if you are a Black Individual resident in America, this book is a must-read for you. Start working on getting healed and breaking the cycle of intergenerational trauma today.

Enjoy!

CHAPTER ONE
What is Trauma?

"Only Human"- Joe Budden

I was 14 years old when we all moved into the house together; my mother, baby brother, stepfather, step-grandmother, and myself. I vividly remember how excited I felt because I was finally getting my own room, on top of not living in an apartment anymore. I showed off our basement to one of my friends, as well as, where I would call my room. He was excited for me because he knew exactly what I experienced living-wise prior to that moment. I thought this was the beginning of a new chapter of happiness, joy, and love; the beginning of our new family! This bliss that I experienced wouldn't last long and this I can say was my first impactful experience with trauma.

My stepfather and his mother started acting as though I was a part of the family and that there was no difference between us even though we were only related through marriage. That shortly changed when whispers began to form about how I was not his biological child and that he didn't have to care for me if he didn't want to. These whispers didn't stop there, they continued into 'I wouldn't amount to anything', that I was a thug because my hair

6

was braided, and that I was a liar. I was convicted of treason on the family that I thought I was a part of and sentenced to be an outcast within the same walls we all were confined to.

My role in the home was to be silent and not heard. My stepfather and step-grandmother made it very clear that I was not one of them and that they thought I was beneath them. At least they did a good job at making me feel like such. The amount of daily emotional abuse and some verbal abuse I experienced led to adverse behaviors. I slept with knives under my pillows thinking that one day they would have had enough of me and try to kill me. I would have nightmares about dying young at the hands of them. I would run away and hoped to never come back. I did not know how to manage my emotions, so I didn't, I bottled them up. My mother tried her best to protect me but she wasn't able to escape the abuse neither. I watched how my brother was treated completely differently from me although I did nothing wrong. This new house that I thought would be filled with happiness, joy, and love was actually missing all three. It was filled with hatred, disgust, and despair all because I simply existed. I turned to my friends for emotional support without telling them what was happening in my home. My family, including my grandmother, provided respite for me and my mother when we tried to escape from the daily trauma we experienced.

This experience impacted me for years after I moved out without me noticing. I couldn't put a name on exactly what I was going through and why I was feeling the way I was feeling even after being released from the confines of that home. It wasn't until I started therapy during graduate school and me telling her my story that she informed me that my experience was traumatic. I actually didn't believe her even though I was learning about this very same thing every day in class. I minimized my experiences due to thinking that "others had it much worse than I did so why am I complaining." This way of thinking exacerbated my symptoms stemming from the trauma I experienced for over 9 years. Once I was able to acknowledge that what occurred was traumatic, I was then able to heal and move forward.

I wanted to share this piece about me to get a slight understanding of what can cause trauma and how it can manifest. Let's now get into some definitions of trauma to build the foundation for what's to come later in the book.

Trauma.

Definition:

It is worthy of note that man will suffer a traumatic event not prepared for at several junctures of life ranging from the loss of a loved one, an assault, an accident, a shocking sight, a natural disaster, or a medical emergency. Additionally, many psychologists and psychiatrists like to remind us of that fact (Exploring your mind, 2018).

As related by the American Psychological Association (APA), trauma is an emotional response to a terrible occurrence like an accident, rape, or natural disaster. However, according to Legg (2020), a person may also experience trauma as a response to any physically or emotionally threatening or harmful event.

Traumatic Events.

An incident that causes physical, spiritual, emotional, or psychological harm is regarded as a traumatic event. As a result, the individual experiencing the unfortunate occurrence may feel threatened, anxious, or frightened. In some cases, the person may not know how to respond or maybe in denial about the effect such an event has had. Therefore, the person will need support and time to recover from the traumatic event and regain emotional and mental stability. Examples of traumatic events include: divorce, war, serious illness, death of a family member, lover, friend, teacher, or pet, physical pain or injury (e.g., severe car accident), natural disasters, moving to a new location, terrorism, parental abandonment, witnessing a death, rape, domestic abuse, prison stay, among others (Cafasso, 2017).

Post-Traumatic Stress Disorder (PTSD).

PTSD develops when there is persistence in the symptoms of trauma after a stressful event. PTSD can result in an intense physical and emotional response to any thought or memory of the event, and it can last for months or years following trauma. It is distressing and interferes with the day-to-day life and relationships of a person (Legg, 2020). PTSD is a type of anxiety confusion that affects stress hormones and changes the body's response to stress.

Its symptoms include severe anxiety, flashbacks, persistent memories of the event, and avoidance behaviors. Risk factors for developing PTSD include previous trauma, having little support after the trauma, physical pain or injury, dealing with other stressors at the same time, such as financial difficulty, and previous anxiety or depression.

Responses to Traumatic Events.

Variations exist in the responses of people who experience traumatic events. Usually, there are no visible signs, but people may have serious emotional reactions. Shock and denial, which are often used to protect oneself from the effects of the emotional impact, experienced shortly after the event is a normal response.

One may feel numb or detached and may not feel the event's full intensity right away.

Common responses to a traumatic event once one has moved past the initial shock include (Cafasso, 2017): anxiety and nervousness, irritability, sudden dramatic mood changes, anger, denial, depression, difficulty concentrating, flashbacks or constant memories of the event, altered sleeping or insomnia, intense fear that the traumatic event will recur, especially around anniversaries of the event (or when going back to the scene of the original event), changes in appetite, withdrawal, and isolation from day-to-day activities, physical symptoms of stress, such as headaches and nausea and worsening of an existing medical condition. Furthermore, a condition known as post-traumatic stress disorder (PTSD) can sometimes occur after one experiences a life-threatening event or witness a death.

Levels of Trauma.

Traumatic events can be isolated or ongoing events. Therefore, the levels of trauma involve (Legg, 2020):

1. Acute trauma: This precipitates from a single stressful or hazardous event.

2. Chronic trauma: This precipitates from repeated and prolonged exposure to increased stressful events. Examples include cases of a child being abused, bullied, or domestically violated.

3. Complex trauma: This precipitates from exposure to multiple traumatic events.

4. Secondary trauma or vicarious trauma: This is another form of trauma where a person (such as family members, mental health care specialists, and others who care for those who have undergone a traumatic event) develops trauma symptoms from close contact with someone undergoing a traumatic event.

Types of Trauma.

There are significantly three ways by which trauma can be specifically categorized, namely (Palwasha, n.d.);

1. Psychological Trauma: These are critical occurrences and out-of-the-norm occasions that occur in a person's life, so overpowering that they regularly become incapacitated, as opposed to setting off a flight-or-fight reaction. Instances of this sort of injury incorporate sexual maltreatment or the suicidal occurrence of a friend or family member. This trauma may result in being related to self-fault, disgrace, shame, or self-loathing.

2. Mass Trauma: Generally, these are traumatic events that are life-threatening and are usually experienced by countless individuals at the same time. Instances of this may incorporate catastrophic events, atomic disasters, psychological oppression, and terrorist circumstances. These circumstances may prompt an expansion in weariness and dread of territory and conditions that trauma happened in.

3. Collective social trauma: These are human-made occasions, normally on account of the state or powerful gatherings. They are frequently classed as exercises done over an extensive period by a group to influence the working of another (often smaller) group over time, to diminish their social impact. These are colonization, war, annihilation, starvation, events that disturb social patterns and customs previously rehearsed. It might deny a collective group of individuals of their power over their networks and lifestyle.

Symptoms of Trauma.

The symptoms of trauma (which could be based on emotional or psychological; physical responses) range from mild to severe (Legg, 2020):

Emotional and psychological symptoms include denial, anger, fear, sadness, shame, confusion, anxiety, depression, numbness, guilt, hopelessness, irritability, difficulty concentrating, sometimes having emotional outbursts, and difficulty coping with feelings; withdrawing from others; and flashbacks.

Physical symptoms that come with emotional reactions are; headaches, digestive symptoms, fatigue, racing heart, sweating, feeling jumpy, and difficulty sleeping.

Causes of Trauma.

The causes of trauma include the following (Legg, 2020); bullying, harassment, physical, psychological, or sexual abuse, sexual assault, traffic collisions, childbirth, life-threatening illnesses, sudden loss of a loved one, being attacked, being kidnapped, acts of terrorism, natural disasters, and war.

Effects of Trauma.

The effects of trauma can be short-term or long-term; that is, a traumatized person can feel a range of emotions right after the event and in the long term. They may become overwhelmed, helpless, shocked, or have difficulty processing their experiences. More so, trauma can have long-term effects on a person's well-being. If symptoms persist and do not reduce in severity, it can point out that the trauma has developed into a mental health disorder referred to as post-traumatic stress disorder (PTSD).

Additionally, trauma has a way of causing someone's parents and parenting to affect how they think and behave into adulthood. Trauma affects the way someone does parenting because it affects things like; the parent's ability to offer a proper child attachment, the exercises a parent decides to do or not do with their child, the stories a parent narrate to a child, the perspective, personal values, and core beliefs a parent teaches the child (Jacobson, 2017).

Factors Influencing the Effects of Trauma.

People have various reactions to traumatic events. For instance, those who live through the same natural disaster can respond very differently despite experiencing the same event. Hence, many factors determine how a traumatic event affects a person. They include (Legg, 2020):

- Their characteristics.
- The type and features of the event(s).
- The presence of other mental health conditions.
- Their background and approach to handling emotions.
- Previous exposure to traumatic events.

Myths and Misconceptions about Trauma.

Even though people realize a lot about trauma, there are still many myths and misconceptions about it. A few of the most popular myths and misconceptions about trauma are (Guest, 2016; Exploring your mind, 2018):

1. Only weak people get post-traumatic stress disorder (PTSD).

Trauma affects everyone differently, and not everyone exposed to a traumatic event will experience post-traumatic stress disorder. Individuals who experience violence are more likely to develop post-traumatic stress disorder than survivors of other types of trauma. Some individuals have a natural resilience or no prior exposure, strong support networks, or effective coping mechanisms; however, their existence does not mean that people who experience post-traumatic stress disorder are weak. Additionally, judging an individual's strength based on their response to trauma is damaging. The focus is supposed to be an understanding of the individual's circumstances and providing an environment that supports recovery.

2. Trauma is a life-sentence that can destroy one's life.

Recovery from trauma is possible. At first, it is very difficult for someone to understand a traumatic event, and in reality, trauma has a dual nature. It presents an undeniably destructive nature that rips apart one's protective bubble, leaving one vulnerable and exposed. On the one hand, however, the bubble can re-form, that is, it transforms people; a little battered though because the wound may not completely heal, but strong enough for one to move on with life and be more able to confront difficulties.

3. It is all bad.

In truth, trauma can lead to growth. It is not unreasonable to presume that a traumatic event is a purely negative one; however, man can integrate these events in a way that can lead to positive changes [Post-traumatic growth (PTG)] with recovery, including new capacities for appreciation and resilience, stronger relationships, deeper spirituality and greater satisfaction with life.

4. Trauma appears after a threatening event.

Trauma does not appear as a reaction to a traumatic event, but rather due to someone's emotional and psychological effect. Besides, sometimes the same event can cause trauma in some people but not in others. When something shocking happens, the traumatic reaction is not immediate. It stems up later after the person begins to question his or her life and reality. For instance, think of a person who has just been diagnosed with cancer. The news at first is enough to make them feel defeated and traumatized; however, for many people, the most striking thing is not always the disease itself, but not having enough support from friends or family.

5. Trauma is a mental illness.

Another misconception is that trauma is a mental illness; however, it is much deeper than that. When someone suffers a psychological trauma, it is also a rupture, and this mental injury makes it impossible for such a person to go back to being who he or she once was (previous state). Hence, a person experiencing trauma is psychologically injured, and those injuries can be moral or emotional.

6. You can deal with trauma alone if you are strong.

The society that we dwell in is one with the belief that only the weak ask for help, such that whoever gets medical assistance is of little or no sense, and strong people can deal with everything without ever breaking down. It is important to note that trauma breaks one inside, and nobody can keep living their lives with a broken soul, a fragmented mind, or an eroded heart regardless of how strong such is.

In the next chapter, we will explore how the events of chattel slavery and other racial traumas have impacted Black people here in America.

CHAPTER TWO
The Historical Trauma of Chattel Slavery in America & Racial Traumatic Events

"Momma"- Kendrick Lamar

I was 19 years old when I took a class called "The Black Power Years." I was on line for Alpha Phi Alpha Fraternity Inc. which further taught me a plethora of Black History during this time in my life. I remember my professor, who was also an Alpha, playing a documentary on Marcus Garvey for the classroom. Initially, I didn't think much of it, as I thought it was just another documentary on a guy who most of us never heard of who may have had a small influence on history. I was wrong! The more I watched this documentary, the angrier I got, and the more I realized that I had been tricked in my education growing up even though my high school was something close to 95% Black. After the documentary was over, I vividly remember saying to myself, "This man had the biggest movement in African American history and I never heard about it until now!" I immediately went to the library and checked out books and began to educate myself on anything and everything related to

Black History. I was stunned, shocked, appalled but empowered to learn more about my people and the Black experience in America. I felt this was exactly where I needed to be at that very point in my life. I was home! This led me to take up the minor of African American studies and that's when I started to learn exactly how brutal Chattel Slavery was in America as well as a documented chronological timeline of racial traumatic events. This leads to the next section of the book; the Black experience in America.

Chattel Slavery in America also considered as a Historical Traumatic Event, should be known as one of the most brutal events that ever took place, not only in American history but the history of the world. Black people were subjected to physical, sexual, emotional, and mental abuse at the highest level for over 300 years. Day in and day out for the majority of their existence, enslaved Blacks were subjected to cruelty, death, and labeled inferior under the guise of false scientific evidence. Once slavery was finally eradicated, Black people were not afforded space for true healing of the wounds of chattel slavery but in fact experienced more trauma, more racial traumatic events.

Racial Traumatic events include race-related or racism-related trauma from occasions or crises experienced or seen by a person. Potential sources would be an individual's personal or group experience of discrimination, racism, and aggression.

Witnessing of extreme exposure to traumatic events also causes trauma, which includes media exposure, such as the prominent killings of people such as;

- Trayvon Martin.
- Ahmaud Aubrey.
- Mike Brown.
- Freddie Gray.
- Eric Gardner.
- Philando Castile.
- Breanna Taylor
- Sandra Bland

Each of these traumatic racial events adds another layer of trauma to the wound that has already been opened by chattel slavery. Let's further dissect chattel slavery and its connection with racial traumatic events.

Chattel Slavery in America.

Black men, women, and children worked from sunup to sundown providing free labor to a society that brutalized them in every way imaginable. They were forced into enslavement to build the economy of America and were captured, beaten, and frequently murdered if they resisted. Women were raped and forced to bear the children of their masters while their husbands watched powerlessly. Children were snatched away from the arms of their mothers and sold as property to fellow slave owners miles away never to be seen again at times. Enslaved Black people were believed to be less than human, subhuman, and savages, who were meant to be treated as such. They were denied basic human rights such as learning how to read and write. Religion; Christianity, was weaponized and forced upon them after they were stripped of their culture and religious beliefs. This form of animalistic behavior and treatment lasted on a group of people for over 300 years without relief or respite. They endured trauma every day of their lives at the hands of those who demonstrated cognitive dissonance and truly believed that they were justified in their actions. Although space for true healing did not follow chattel slavery, it must be noted that the resilience displayed by those who were enslaved and afterward is something like we've never seen before. However, that resilience did not stop the trauma responses that continued to be passed down in our communities and our families to this day. We will look at the history of the Black experience in America post-slavery so that we can get a better understanding of how Racial Traumatic events have continued to occur over healing.

Black Codes.

The Black Codes, at times referred to as Black Laws, were laws governing African Americans (free Blacks). The most popular of them was passed in 1865 and 1866 by Southern states, after the American Civil War, to confine African Americans' freedom and force them to work for low wages. Black codes were prohibitive laws intended to restrict the opportunity of African Americans and guarantee their accessibility as a cheap labor force after slavery. Although Black Codes existed before the Common War and numerous Northern states had them, it was the Southern U.S. states that arranged such laws in regular practice. Despite the fact that the Union victory had given nearly 4 million enslaved Black people their freedom, the subject of liberating Blacks' status in the postwar South was still particularly uncertain. Under Black codes, numerous states expected Blacks to sign yearly work contracts; if they disagree, they risk being captured, fined, and constrained into unpaid work. The outrage over Black codes sabotaged support for President Andrew Johnson and the Republican Party.

In 1832, James Kent composed that, "In the majority of the US, there is a differentiation in regard to political benefits, between free white people and free Black people of African blood; and in no aspect of the nation do the Blacks, in the purpose of certainty, take an interest similarly with the whites, in the activity of common and political rights" (Kent, 1832).

Ever since colonial time, colonies and states had passed laws that oppressed free Blacks. In the South, these were commonly added to the "slave codes;" the objective was to lessen the impact of free Blacks (especially after slave uprisings) because of their likely influence on slaves. Limitations included disallowing them from casting their votes (albeit North Carolina had permitted this before 1831), carrying weapons, gathering in groups for worship, and being educated with the ability to read and write. Before the war, Northern states that had banned slavery likewise enacted laws like the slave codes and the later Black Codes: Illinois, New York, Ohio, Michigan, and Connecticut established laws to debilitate free Blacks from living in those states. They were denied equivalent political rights, including the right to cast a vote, go to state-funded schools, and receive the same treatment under the law. They likewise controlled where they lived, how they traveled, and seized their children for labor purposes. A portion of the Northern states which had those laws in place revoked them around the same period that the Civil War ended, and slavery was nullified by constitutional amendment.

During the first two years after the Civil War, Southern legislatures, which were white-dominated, passed Black Codes demonstrated after the former slave codes. The name "Black Codes" was bestowed by "Negro pioneers and the Republican organs," as indicated by history specialist, John S. Reynolds (Reynolds, 1905). Black Codes were essential for a larger white pattern attempting to keep up political predominance and smother the freedmen, recently liberated African American slaves. They were especially worried about controlling freedmen's development and work, as a free labor framework had supplanted slavery. Even though freedmen had been liberated, their lives were incredibly limited by the Black Codes.

The characterizing feature of the Black Codes was expansive vagrancy law, which permitted local authorities to arrest freed individuals for minor infractions and commit them to involuntary labor.

Jim Crow laws.

Jim Crow laws were known as a collection of state and local resolutions that sanctioned racial segregation. It was named after a Black entertainer show character. The laws existed for around 100 years, from the post-Civil War period until 1968. The laws were intended to marginalize African Americans by denying them the option to cast a vote, get jobs, education, or other opportunities to better their lives. The individuals who opposed Jim Crow laws faced arrest, fines, prison sentences, brutality, and deaths frequently. Just as the national Democratic Party and President Andrew Johnson, the local governments frustrated efforts to help Black Americans push ahead. Brutality was on the rise, making dangers become a regular part of African American life. Black schools were vandalized and crushed, and groups of violent white individuals assaulted, tormented, and lynched Black residents in the night. Families were assaulted and constrained off their territory all over the South.

The most savage association of the Jim Crow time, the Ku Klux Klan (KKK), was conceived in 1865 in Pulaski, Tennessee, as an exclusive hangout for Confederate veterans. The KKK developed into a secret society threatening African American populations and seeping through white Southern culture, with their members at the most significant government levels and in the least echelons of criminal back alleys.

In the early 1880s, large urban communities in the South were not completely under obligation to Jim Crow laws, and Black Americans discovered more opportunities in them. These discoveries prompted considerable Black populaces to move to the urban areas, and, as the decade advanced, white city inhabitants requested more laws to restrict open doors for African Americans. Before long, Jim Crow laws spread around the nation with significantly more power than beforehand. Public parks were taboo for African Americans to enter, and theaters and cafés were isolated. Isolated lounge areas in transport and train stations were required, just as water fountains, bathrooms, building doors, lifts, graveyards, even relaxation places. Laws prohibited African Americans from living in white neighborhoods. Isolation was authorized for public pools, telephone corners, medical clinics, refuges, correctional facilities, and private homes for the old and handicapped.

A few states required separate course books for Black and white students. In Atlanta, Black People were given a Bible different from that of the whites to swear to in court. Marriage and living together among whites and Blacks was strictly illegal in most Southern states. It was usual to see signs posted at town and city limits cautioning African Americans that they were not welcome there.

As oppressive as the Jim Crow period seemed to be, it was when numerous African Americans around the nation ventured forward into leadership positions to contradict those laws vigorously. Some of them were; Ida B. Wells, a Memphis teacher who became co-owner of the Memphis Free Speech and Headlight, utilized her position to take on school segregation and sexual harassment.

Charlotte Hawkins Brown, a North Carolina-born, Massachusetts-raised Black woman who began fundraising to start her school, named the Palmer Memorial Institute. She was the first Black woman to create a Black school in North Carolina, and through her education work, she became a fierce and vocal opponent of Jim Crow laws.

Isaiah Montgomery, who was formerly enslaved, created the African American-only town of Mound Bayou, Mississippi, in 1887. He enlisted other former enslaved people to settle in the wilderness with him, clearing the land and forging a settlement that incorporated several schools, an Andrew Carnegie-funded library, three cotton gins, a bank, a hospital, and a sawmill. Mound Bayou is still in existence today and is still almost 100 percent Black.

Although the Jim Crow laws were technically off the books, that has not always guaranteed full integration or adherence to anti-racism laws throughout the United States of America.

Mass Lynching.

Throughout the late 19th century period, racial tension grew all over the United States. A greater amount of this strain was noticeable in the Southern parts of the United States. In the south, individuals blamed their financial issues on the newly freed slaves who lived around them. Lynching turned into a popular way of resolving some of the anger that whites had concerning the free Blacks.

In early 1919, white-on-Black brutality erupted in thirty-six United States cities lasting through the summer and into the fall of that year. James Weldon Johnson, an activist for civil rights, and the author referred to it as the "Red Summer."

In Chicago, violence broke out from 27 July to 3 August 1919, when a Black American child, Eugene Williams, unintentionally swam into a whites-only swimming region at a beach near 29th street. A white beachgoer started throwing rocks at Eugene, causing him to drown. When the Black beachgoers who witnessed the assault began to complain, they were assaulted by the whites. The violence rapidly spilled into the streets like wildfire, and white mobs started launching attacks into Black neighborhoods. As the situation kept on escalating, the Chicago Police Department rarely intervened. By the time the brutality ended, 537 people were injured, 38 were executed, and up to 2,000 individuals, mostly Black, lost their homes (Jed, 2020).

In Washington, D.C., violence broke out from 19 July to 24 July 1919. It started in the wake of a rumor that a Black man had forcefully violated a white woman. White men, many of whom had experience in the military, launched into mob attacks on Black individuals and organizations. The Washington D.C. Police Department refused to get involved, forcing the Black residents of D.C. to retaliate to protect themselves. After four days of police inactivity, Woodrow Wilson beckoned on 2,000 federal troops to quell the city. In the aftermath of the rampage, 150 people had been injured, and 15 were killed (Jed, 2020).

Similar outbreaks of racially motivated violence broke out in cities across the nation. However, the largest mass lynching or red summer in American history occurred in the fall of 1919. White mobs descended on a rural Phillips County, Arkansas community and engaged in African Americans' wholesale slaughter. The failure to win the Civil War and the annulment of slavery did little to curtail Southern plantation owners' greed and racism. They, in no time, reestablished slavery under the guise of sharecropping. The previous enslaved Black people had been guaranteed land in the wake of the Civil War; however, the government quickly reneged on the promise.

With no land and being confronted with overwhelming racism at every turn, the former slaves were left with barely any choices. They were exploited by the plantation owners who ensnared the previous slaves in sharecropping contracts. The landowners manipulated the contracts to the disadvantage of the former slaves. They withheld pricing and data sale from the sharecroppers and underpaid them for their labor. The plantation owners developed loans to the sharecroppers they underpaid, shackling them with debt. It was a usual practice called peonage, which had been prohibited by law since 1867. The Civil War prohibited slavery, but it did nothing to change racism against Blacks. The plantation owners showed a lack of respect for the law against peonage, and the government, which was also racist after the war as in the past, did little to enforce the law.

On 30 September 1919, three miles north of Elaine, Arkansas, about 100 Black People in America were assembled in a small church referred to as "Hoop Spur." Most individuals present were sharecroppers, and some had returned the winter before from the war in Europe. They posted armed guards to shield the gathering from outrage or interference by the white plantation owners. The Red Summer was national news, they were aware of the violence against Blacks nationwide, and they were present at this church for a gathering that would most likely visit this outrage upon them.

They had been utilized unfairly by the white plantation owners who underpaid them for their crops while positioning them deeply into debt, leasing to the condition of peonage. They had made plans to retaliate against this exploitation and other grievances by forming a union. The group was called "Progressive Farmers and Household Union of America," and it was set up by Robert Hill, a Black tenant farmer from Winchester, Arkansas. This effort to unite was vigorously opposed by the white plantation owners and people in the business. They started spying on the meetings and trying to interpose as much as possible. On this particular night, Charles Pratt, Phillips County deputy, and W.D. Atkins, a white railroad police officer, had been sent to the church to break up the gathering. Shots were exchanged, and Charles Pratt was severely wounded, while W.D. Atkins was killed.

The plantation owners and business people found out the Black sharecroppers were making plans to pursue fair pay for seeking crops, pursuing litigation, and putting together their money in a common effort to buy their land to break free of the sharecropping system. However, the white businessmen and plantation owners, having practiced years of illegal peonage and other shady practices, resorted to racially motivated brutality against the African American farmers in a bid to silence them.

On 1 October 1919, the day following the shooting incident that happened in the church, the post members were summoned to the courthouse due to the assassination of Special Agent Adkins near Elaine. Among those reacting were James A. Tappan, Clinton Lee, and Ira Proctor. They were among the first individuals to show up on the murder scene and subsequent fighting with Negro rioters. James and Clinton were killed, and Ira Proctor was seriously wounded. The Sheriff of Phillips County had planned a posse to capture the men who were at the church. The American members served in the posse on this first day, and some led additional mobs in the days that followed. As indicated in a timeline by the University of Arkansas, during the early morning periods of 1 October, reports of African Americans assaulting the whites spread all over the Delta region, on both sides of the Mississippi River. During the day, some 500–1000 armed men came down upon Phillips County from all over. Among these armed men were the members of the Ku Klux Klan (KKK) and other militant organizations. According to white eyewitnesses, they began butchering Blacks, shooting them without hesitation, who later testified in affidavits.

A deputy related that Elaine was under attack by a group of Black rioters. Regardless of the report, no white casualties were mentioned. The Arkansas Gazette reported, "At least fifteen Black men were lying in the streets and outskirts of the town and that more would also be found in the woods." Other reports mention that the dead African Americans' bodies were mutilated, and body parts were removed as souvenirs. Homes of Black Individuals in America were ransacked and looted after many had fled their houses to hide in the countryside regions, fearing for their lives. No assault on white farmers and other residents in the area was described. Throughout the day, more African

Americans were killed or arrested as the mobs hunted them down.

The next day, Arkansas Governor Brough, had requested assistance from the U.S. War Department came with 500 soldiers and 12 machine guns under the command of Colonel Isaac Jenks, and followed by Governor Brough, arrived by train in the town of Elaine. They tried to disarm everyone, both whites, and Blacks, covering up all that had happened. African American survivors were told to return to work and act as if nothing had occurred. Over the following weeks, editorials were published in Arkansas and surrounding states warning Black individuals to avoid further agitation under the threat of more deaths.

From the period of October through November 1919, a grand jury was convened in Phillips County, and charges involving murder were brought against 122 African Americans. No whites were ever charged. 65 of the 122 men entered pleas of not guilty as they were under threat of the death penalty and afraid for their lives. Therefore, they were sentenced to twenty-one years in prison. Of the remaining men, their cases continued hearing at the court, and some were able to have their cases turned off due to lack of proof. Near the end of November 1919, twelve men remained who faced the death penalty.

Jared Washington

Red Lining.

Red Lining refers to a discriminatory pattern of disinvestment and obstructive loaning practices that hinder homeownership among Black People in America and other people of color. It was the practice of outlining zones with sizable Black populaces in red ink on maps as a notice to mortgage lenders, effectively segregating Black people in areas that would suffer lower investment levels than their white counterparts. Banks utilized the concept to deny loans to homeowners and would-be homeowners who lived in these neighborhoods. Thus, this brought about neighborhood economic decline and the retention of services or their provision at an exceptionally high expense.

The root of the term originates from the policies that were created by the Home Owners Loan Corporation (HOLC) setup in 1933 by the Franklin Roosevelt Administration to decrease home foreclosures during the rejection and after that, was institutionalized by the 1937 U.S. Housing Act, which set up the Federal Housing Association (FHA). Federal agencies for housing, including the HOLC and the FHA, determined whether zones were deemed unsuitable for investment by banks, insurance organizations, savings and loan corporations, and other financial services companies. The regions were physically demarcated with red shading on a map. Conversely, areas that were to receive preferential lending status were lined in green shading and intermediate zones in blue shading. Usually, these decisions were arbitrarily founded on the region's racial composition rather than income levels. While the practice was practically widespread before 1968, the Civil Rights Act passed theoretically prohibited redlining. Nevertheless, its impact was felt long after that date.

As a result of redlining, neighborhoods that local banks esteemed as unsuitable for investment were left underdeveloped or in decay. Attempts to improve these zones with even relatively small-scale business ventures were often deterred by financial institutions that kept on labeling the underwriting as too hazardous or simply rejected them altogether. When the initially established businesses collapsed, new ones were not allowed to replace them, leaving the entire blocks empty and disintegrating. Consequently, African Americans in those neighborhoods were often restricted to banking, retail merchandise, healthcare, and even groceries. A prominent exception to this was (and still is) the expansion of liquor stores and bars, which transcended the zone's stigma of financial risk. Also, redlining led to an appreciable deficiency of employment opportunities in these zones as prospective small-scale employers were unwilling to situate there. Crime frequently continued in the wake of these declining neighborhoods, thereby making future investment more outlandish.

Today, these redlined zones totally remain more isolated and economically disadvantaged, with higher Black and minority portions of the populace than the rest of the city.

Moreover, they have lower median household income, lower home values, older housing stock, and rents, which are lesser in absolute terms (but often higher as a percentage of income).

Tuskegee Syphilis Experiment.

It is otherwise called the Tuskegee Experiment. The Tuskegee Experiment of Untreated Syphilis in the Black Men in America was a clinical study held between the years 1932 and 1972 by the United States Public Health Service (PHS). The reason for this study was to observe the characteristic history of untreated syphilis; the African American men in the examination were just told that they were getting free medical care from the Federal Government of the United States. The examination started when there was no known treatment for the ailment. The PHS began the investigation in 1932 as a team with Tuskegee University (initially known as the Tuskegee Institute), a Black college in Alabama. Researchers made use of 600 impoverished African American sharecroppers from Macon County, Alabama. Of these men, 399 had syphilis, with a control group of 201 men who were not infected at all (CDC, 2020). The men were guaranteed free medical care as an incentive for participating in the study. However, they were misled by the PHS, who camouflaged fake treatments, ineffective strategies, and diagnostic procedures as treatment. The men who had syphilis were never educated regarding their diagnosis, despite the danger of infecting others, and the way that the ailment could prompt visual impairment, deafness, psychological maladjustment, coronary illness, bone disintegration, breakdown of the focal sensory system, and death.

As stated by the administration concerned with diseases, the Center for Disease Control and Prevention, the men were only told that they were being treated for what is referred to as "bad blood," a term that described various states of infirmities such as syphilis, anemia, and fatigue. "Bad blood" was a major cause of death within the southern African American community. Initially, the men were told that the study would only take place for six months, but it was extended to 40 years. After the funding for treatment was used up, the study was continued without informing the men that they would never be treated. In 1947, penicillin, an antibiotic, had become the standard treatment for syphilis, but none of the infected men were treated with it (Duff-Brown, 2017).

The study's clinicians could have decided to treat every syphilitic subject, close the investigation, or split off a control group to test with penicillin. Rather, they proceeded with the examination without treating any members; they retained treatment and data about it from the subjects. Also, researchers kept members from getting to syphilis treatment programs accessible to other occupants in the area. The 40-year Study of Untreated Syphilis in the African American Male was a major infringement of moral standards. Researchers intentionally failed to treat participants appropriately after penicillin was proven viable for syphilis and became widely available (Duff-Brown, 2017). Additionally, those participants remained ignorant of the study clinicians' actual purpose, which was to observe the natural course of untreated syphilis.

During the 1960s, a PHS venereal disease investigator in San Francisco named Peter Buxton discovered the Tuskegee study and communicated his concerns to his bosses that it was unethical. Accordingly, PHS authorities surveyed the experiment. As a result of the experiment's findings, which had led to many deaths, Buxton leaked out the story to a journalist friend, who gave it to another reporter, Jean Heller of the Associated Press. Heller broke the story in July 1972, inciting public shock and compelling the study to close down on 16 November of the same year. This disclosure prompted significant changes in U.S. law and guidelines concerning the protection of participants in clinical studies. The victims of the experiment, all African Americans, included 28 participants who had died from syphilis, 100 more who had died from related complications. Also, 40 spouses of these participants were diagnosed with the disease, and 19 children were brought into the world with congenital syphilis (Nix, 2019).

In 1973, Congress conducted hearings on the Tuskegee experiments. The subsequent year the study's surviving participants and the families of those who died received a $10 million out-of-court settlement. On 16 May 1997, President Bill Clinton formally apologized on behalf of the United States to the study victims. However, many African Americans still possess a lingering and deep mistrust of public health officials due to the Tuskegee experiment.

Mass Incarceration and Police brutality.

Recently, there has been the killing of George Floyd, an African American man, at the hands of a white police officer in Minneapolis, and this has raised mass protests across the globe. George Floyd was asphyxiated to death as the cop, without shame or hesitation, knelt on his neck for nine long minutes. Do you wonder what his crime was? Counterfeiting a $20 note. While this occurrence unveiled the systemically-rooted leftovers of racism that continue to exist in the 21st century, it also featured the dehumanization faced by Black people at the hands of law enforcement personnel in the United States (U. S. Black people are brutalized within justice and prison systems and the state capitalizes on their incarceration. It is no exaggeration to call the U.S. prison system an 'ethno racial ghetto'. Today, there are more Black Individuals in America in prison than in college (Mallory, 2015). The present incarceration policies strongly reflect the legacies of slavery that have long plagued the nation's social and moral fabric. Marginalized communities keep suffering at the hands of a justice system that paradoxically metes out injustice.

Black Americans, the first victims of mass incarceration programs, are constantly enslaved by way of racist laws and stereotypes that brand them as 'problematic' residents. Although the Civil War marked the abolition of slavery in the United States, "Through the 13th Amendment to the U.S. Constitution (allowing forced labor in prison) and various other legal practices, the current prison system has shown itself into an institution of forced labor, consisting of people of colour" (Raza, 2011, p.159). Human Rights Watch reported in 2000 that 'the Blacks constitute 13 percent of all the users of drugs, but 35 percent of those captured for drug possession, 55 percent of those convicted of the case, and 74 percent of those sent to prison'(Small, 2001). While the 2010 Fair Sentencing Act somewhat eased this disparity, much remains to be done to undo the damage suffered by Black communities across centuries. (Carlsen, 2010). Racial profiling fuelled by stereotypes that Black individuals are more liable to drug use has also played against the population of Black People in America, who have been relentlessly halted and searched by police, and too often, injured or murdered in the processes. Black male adults are close to five times more susceptible to being unfairly stopped and three times more susceptible to being searched by police officers than their white counterparts (Desilver, Lipka, and Fahmy, 2020). While the annulment of slavery more than 150 years ago elevated non-white individuals to the same ground under the law on paper, law enforcement divisions, working together hand in hand with the system of justice, continue to enslave them to date.

Again, race has a strong bearing on convictions, wherein a large number of Black Individuals in America and Latinos are wrongfully convicted for crimes, even when prima facie proofs suggest otherwise. In an issue that later came to be acknowledged as the 'Central Park Five', five young Black men were unjustly convicted in 1989 for a sexual violation they never committed through forced confessions. Only in 2002, when the men's lives had been ruined and slandered by national violence, did another murderer confess to having perpetrated the rape (Duru, 2004). This injustice done is also quantifiable: an innocent Black person is seven times more prone to being convicted for murder than an innocent white person (Gross, Possley, and Stephens, 2017).

Such dehumanizing treatment and outrage contributed to higher rates of recidivism. Even after being freed from jail, 1 out of 4 people is arrested again within the same year. These are usually people whose problems, such as substance abuse and mental illness, have been exacerbated during and after incarceration. The system stunts and sabotages the growth of prisoners instead of rehabilitating them, and because Blacks are so highly incarcerated, this affects the entirety of the African American community. The prison abolition movement argues for a different approach to crime, one that frees itself 'from the assumption that punishment must be a necessary reaction to all violations of the law' (Davis and Rodriguez, 2000) and rather envisions reformative justice accomplished through other methods of rehabilitation.

We have provided the foundation by dissecting trauma and the history of the Black experience in America. Next, we will dive deep into what exactly Intergenerational trauma is to further explore its impact on Black people.

CHAPTER THREE
What is Intergenerational Trauma?

"Be Free"- J. Cole

I remember being 10 years when the murder of Amadou Diallo by 4 police officers took place in New York City. Being from New Jersey, I'm quite sure our news coverage was saturated with this case due to proximity. The memories regarding the details of this case are vague and spotty but what remains is the message it sent me, my family, and other Black people around the country, once again. This message was that people who looked like me, Black people, can be murdered at the hands of police and consequences do not follow. This message of no matter how innocent you are, as a Black person, you are held to a different standard when being approached and confronted by police. This message isn't new, nor has it faded since that time when I was 10 years old. This was my first memorable lesson on Racial Traumatic events. Many of us who identify as Black in America may share similar experiences.

Additionally, I remember the messages my mother told me growing up, as it related to police officers. "When you're being pulled over keep your hands on the steering wheel. Make sure you don't reach for anything too fast," etc. What was happening was my mother passing down a mentality based on survival, through storytelling, which can be labeled as a trauma response from her generation to mine. This trauma response can be traced back to having connections to Chattel Slavery that continues to be passed down in our community and families and further reinforced today by Racial Traumatic events like Amadou Diallo.

My mother was only doing what she was taught by her mother, who was taught by her mother as well through first-hand experience. The likelihood of me teaching these same messages to my daughters are far greater than I want. This is Intergenerational Trauma! I do believe though, that there is a sense of healing that can be passed down with these messages instead of only trauma. The question is how do we pass down healing from such traumatic events that continue to happen today? Although we hope to explore that question with possible answers, let's further dissect and break down Intergenerational Trauma.

Definition

Intergenerational trauma can be described as a collective complex trauma inflicted on individuals who share a specified group identity or affiliation; nationality, ethnicity, and religious affiliation. It is the legacy of multiple traumatic events a community experiences over generations (Winter, 2012).

Generally, intergenerational trauma refers to how trauma experienced in one generation affects future generations' health and well-being (Dekel and Goldblatt, 2008; Bezo and Maggi, 2015). Simply put, intergenerational trauma refers to trauma that passes through or can be transferred in between generations (Jacobson, 2017). The idea or brain behind Intergenerational trauma is that not only can someone experience trauma, but they can then transmit the symptoms and behaviors of trauma survival on to their children, who might further transmit these along the family line. That is, it describes the impact of a traumatic experience, not only on one generation but on subsequent generations after the event via complex post-traumatic stress disorder mechanisms. Intergenerational trauma is a psychological term, and it is also referred to as 'Transgenerational trauma' (Jacobson, 2017; King-White, 2020).

Furthermore, for a complete discussion on intergenerational trauma, it is expedient to consider historical events that may have a long-lasting effect on generations to come; hence, historical trauma.

Historical Trauma.

Historical trauma is a form of intergenerational trauma. In contrast, intergenerational trauma is within a family, and historical trauma also referred to as 'collective trauma' affects many individuals or even an entire generation' that is, it entails instances of intergenerational trauma where the trauma is a shared occurrence among a group of individuals and their role in society (Jacobson, 2017). The Administration for Children and Families explained that historical trauma (such as the Holocaust, displacement, famine, natural disaster, war, terrorism, and slavery) is an intergenerational trauma experienced by a specific cultural group with a history of suffering from systemic oppression, more specifically known as genocide (Jacobson, 2017; King-White, 2020).

Generally, historical trauma consists of three factors (O'Neill et al., 2018):

- The widespread nature;

- Traumatic events resulting in collective suffering, and

- The evil intent of those inflicting the trauma.

This form of trauma is important as it affects a large populace and is typically more complex than individual trauma. Historical trauma can lead to a greater loss of identity and definition. It can have a cumulative effect that reverberates across generations and the society at large in the form of emotional, psychological, and even physical trauma if left unaddressed (Eyerman, 2004).

History of Intergenerational Trauma.

The concept of intergenerational transmission of trauma was developed from research on Jewish Holocaust survivors. Intergenerational trauma was first recognized in the children of Holocaust survivors. In 1966, psychologists began to observe many children of Holocaust survivors seeking mental help in clinics in Canada. The grandchildren of Holocaust survivors were overrepresented among the referrals to a psychiatry clinic compared to their representation in the general population (Fossion et al., 2003). Since then, transgenerational trauma has been documented in descendants of enslaved Africans, Native Americans, war survivors, refugees, survivors of interpersonal abuse, and many other groups. More so, research shows that trauma is shared across generations through a variety of ways, including gene expression, socialization, and psychological disposition. While the source of trauma may be distant, the effects can still be devastating to children (Long, 2020).

Identification of Intergenerational Trauma.

The signs of intergenerational trauma can pose difficult to notice, but three things can help one in identifying if a child may need help (Long, 2020):

- A knowledge of vulnerable populations;

- An understanding of common PTSD symptoms in children; and

- A readiness to create a safe space for a child.

Vulnerable Groups of Intergenerational Trauma.

In addition to descendants of Holocaust survivors, populations that are vulnerable to intergenerational trauma include (Long, 2020; King-White, 2020):

- Any family.

- Refugees.

- Native Americans and indigenous peoples.

- Descendants of Enslaved Africans.

Causes of Intergenerational Trauma.

A classic example of intergenerational trauma is childhood abuse (e.g., sexual, physical, or emotional) that causes a chain of abuse and anxiety in ongoing generations. Other types of trauma or traumatic events that could cause intergenerational trauma include; extreme poverty, parental incarceration, divorce, alcohol use disorder, immediate or violent death of a family member, a crime against a relative, a parent who fought in a war, and torture of a family member, and likes. (Jacobson, 2017; King-White, 2020).

Symptoms of Intergenerational Trauma.

Individuals exhibit varying reactions to traumatic events and often do not realize the effects of the event(s). Intergenerational trauma symptoms may vary based on families' experiences, physical, emotional, or behavioral. More so, the symptoms suffered by some family members could be associated with Post Traumatic Stress Disorder (PTSD).

Symptoms of intergenerational trauma may involve but are not restricted to (King-White, 2020): denial, depersonalization, memory loss, nightmares, psychic numbing, isolation, hyper-vigilance, substance abuse, identification with the death, unresolved grief, lack of trust of others, anger, fearfulness, irritability, and inability to connect with others.

Illustrations Regarding Intergenerational Trauma.

Illustration 1

Consider a sexually abused mother, who hasn't sought support to deal with her trauma. She suffers from symptoms of hyper-vigilance, anxiety, low self-esteem, repressed anger, inconsistent moods, depression, damaged sense of self or lack of identity, paranoia, and even ongoing health issues where she is always experiencing tiredness and has colds/flu (all symptoms of complex post-traumatic stress disorder).

She desires to love her child, but she is often so stressed out and feels so unhappy (depression). And at times, she is just miles away without meaning to be (dissociation), all leading to a child with attachment issues. In truth, she often does not know who she is, or if life has a point. But now she is a mother, and he is her reason for living and source of happiness (codependency/over parenting/domineering parenting). Whenever her child does good, she tells him what an angel he is, and when he is not an angel, she locks herself in her room for a few hours (emotional unavailability due to trauma).

At other times, she tells him stories about her life. How difficult it was, how she learned to not believe anyone or anything. How unfortunate her luck was, but that is just the way life is (transmitting anxiety via stories). She does try to keep her child safe, like not allowing him to play ice hockey. It is far too risky. And she makes sure that when she goes into the shops, he is in the car, locked in (transmitting anxiety and negative core beliefs).

Like you can imagine, the child of such parenting will themselves have anxiety, hyper-vigilance, possible low self-esteem (all signs of post-traumatic stress disorder), or anxiety disorders (Jacobson, 2017).

Illustration 2

In the 1930s and '40s, LaVerne Daisy Miller's mother and seven siblings were placed in foster care in New York City. Their experiences in regards to these placements were unimaginable, Miller explains. By the time they had grown into adulthood and leaving the foster care system, they were what many would refer to as survivors.

However, surviving does not mean coming out unhurt. The experience of foster care left longing impressions on Miller's mother, aunts, and uncles. Miller saw first-hand the effects it had on her mother as a parent. "She was hyper-vigilant," Miller says. "She had a lack of limitations and was actually heavily involved in our personal lives in a way that a parent should not be. Her identity was all linked up to our failures and successes. For a long period, I did not know where my mother ended and I started." Her mother seemed to lack the ability to be openly tenderhearted and still does. "At the age of 53, I will still ask my mother, 'Why don't you say you love me?' It is difficult for her to express that."

Miller, a lawyer and co-director of the Substance Abuse and Mental Health Services Administration–funded statewide Family and Consumer Network Technical Assistance Centre, adds that she has begun to notice how the effects of her mother's experiences have affected her parenting. "I think one of my underlying difficulties is my inability to express kindness in an outward way," she would say. "I can send out a note or a card or a mountain of cards." But anything beyond the notes and cards is hard. "That affects my son because I'm not around in ways he would like me to be."

"Another thing is that I'm most times very overprotective," she added. "I do not want him to hurt or experience the hurts that I have. At times I overcompensate." Miller also added that her mother did the best that she could, and though she does not say it, it is evident that Miller has. However, the effects of her mother's experiences continue to affect Miller, Miller's son, and potentially generations to come (Coyle, 2014).

Summarily, both illustrations depict how trauma does not always vanish in its effects but rather, can trickle down from generation to generation. This type of trauma, called intergenerational or historical trauma, can affect a family, a community, or people depending on its reach or scope.

Now that we have examined the definition of Intergenerational Trauma, let's further dissect how it is passed down.

CHAPTER FOUR
The Generational Transmission of Trauma

"DNA."- Kendrick Lamar

W as in my final classes of graduate school when they extended the program to include 4 more courses for students who may want to get their full counselor license out of the state of Georgia. I took my school up on that offer because at the time I didn't think I would be staying in Georgia much longer after I graduated. Nonetheless, I took a class that specifically focused on trauma. I thoroughly enjoyed this course because it gave me a more comprehensive understanding of what trauma is and how to treat individuals who struggle from trauma. The books we read were some of the popular books that circulate the mental health field regarding trauma. If you haven't already picked up on this earlier in the book as I recounted some of my experiences as it relates to African American history, I am a lover of everything Black. I consider myself a social justice activist and fight for equity for Black people. With that being said, this experience is where I learned exactly how my Clinical

Mental Health Counseling degree would be used to impact Black people.

One day sitting in class, my professor was discussing how trauma manifests in different individuals and how trauma can be passed down through generations. This immediately intrigued me. My thoughts almost automatically went to, "if trauma can be passed down through generations, how does that relate to Black people in America?" I sat there processing that concept because to me I felt like I finally connected the dots as it relates to the Black experience in America. I quickly shot my hand up and was called on to speak, I responded with exactly what I was thinking, "If trauma can be passed down through different generations, then is it safe to say that Black people in America could very well be experiencing trauma responses stemming from slavery?" She paused for a second and said, "Yes that is possible." Although she thought it was "possible" I thought it was fact and reality. This energized me and I began my research in Intergenerational Trauma before I could name it. That's when I learned exactly how the transmission of trauma can actually happen. This is when I found out my purpose and why I was created. At this point, you "Couldn't tell me nothing." Here in this chapter of the book, we will explore the general transmission of trauma through different generations in a family and community.

Transmission of Trauma.

Traumatic encounters can be transferred physiologically, environmentally, and socially (Zur Foundation, 2014). Grown-up children with parents determined to have Post Traumatic Stress Disorder (PTSD) regularly portray damaged, distracted parents who were emotionally not accessible when required. In a year, many children are exposed to traumatic occurrences that sway them and the generations to come. The presentation to intergenerational trauma can affect children for a lifetime. Consequently, it is appropriate to know the different manners by which trauma can be moved, starting with one generation then onto the next. A pattern of trauma, where its effect is transmitted from one generation then onto the next, is made through (Mending Establishment, 2020; Zaman, 2020; Lord White, 2020):

Epigenetics in the DNA.

Epigenetics is explained as the study of the changes in organisms, which are brought about by altering gene expression instead of modifying the genetic code itself. Trauma can leave a chemical marking on an individual's genes, which would then be passed down to people in the future. This imprint doesn't cause a genetic mutation, yet it modifies the process by which the gene is expressed. This change isn't hereditary but epigenetic. DNA alterations can affect the activity of the gene without changing the actual sequence of DNA. Epigenetic changes are the chemical compounds that are added to single genes that influence their action. Since these chemical substances are connected to the DNA, they remain, even as the cells undergo division; this implies that they can be gone down through ages.

According to a physician and neuroscientist, Ali Jawaid, his observation on some children in the orphanages in Pakistan that experienced the war with their parents. It was sent down to the orphanage home. They provide the best possible support of shelter and health care and send kids to local schools. However, these children experience symptoms similar to PTSD (post-traumatic stress disorder), including anxiety and depression (Andrew, 2019). According to Andrew (2019), with some proof from his research, genetic variations could then be passed down between generations, predisposing their recipients to be sensitive to ensuing traumas and stressors.

Notwithstanding the potential genetic changes that children may have acquired from traumatized parents and grandparents, Black Americans additionally manage mental and social sources of trauma that are passed starting with one age then onto the next. The person's parents or grandparents may have tales about how their family members endure the Jim Crow period, set apart by the White community's terror and dread. There are great deals of messages passed on at an early age that position Black people to accept that the world is an undermining place. Yet, when you are a child, you attempt to comprehend your place in the world;

being plunged with these messages; that are defensive from various perspectives is exceptionally traumatic.

According to a discussion with Dr. Chris Mason, Associate Professor at Weill Cornell Medicine, and Director of the Mason Lab, epigenetics, is simply studying the biological control systems of DNA. It is the light switches that turn on or off the genes. Fundamentally, this infers that; epigenetics controls how or why your genes are expressed (Erdelyi, 2020). Presently, the opinion that an individual's encounter could modify their children and grandchildren's biology and conduct has gained an increased attraction. Animals and some little human examinations have indicated that exposure to stressors like enormous pressure or cold can trigger subsequent generations' metabolic changes. Dr. Mason explained that the field of epigenetics gained an increased foothold about some years ago, when researchers distributed a fundamental examination on the Dutch Hunger Winter, an all-encompassing time of starvation that occurred as World War II was ending when the Nazis hindered food supplies in October 1944, pushing a great part of the Netherlands into starvation. When the Dutch were freed in May 1945, more than 20,000 had died due to starvation. Pregnant women were especially vulnerable to this event, and the starvation affected the unborn children for the rest of their lives.

Researchers found that the individuals who had been in existence during the famine were a couple of pounds heavier than normal. (The reasoning goes that the moms, since they were starving, consequently calmed a gene in their unborn kids engaged with consuming the body's fuel.) When the children reached their middle ages, they had higher LDL ("bad") cholesterol and triglyceride levels. They additionally endured higher paces of obesity, diabetes, cardiovascular diseases, and schizophrenia. Researchers investigated why they found that these children conveyed a particular chemical imprint, an epigenetic signature on one of their genes.

Dr. Rachel Yehuda, the Director of Traumatic Stress Studies Division at the Icahn School of Medicine, Mount Sinai, New York City, conducted a report on 40 Holocaust survivors' offspring. She discovered that they had epigenetic changes to a gene connected to their cortisol levels, a hormone engaged with the stress response. She likewise found an unmistakable pattern of DNA methylation, another epigenetic marker. The investigation inferred that both parents and their unborn kids were influenced on a genetic level. While many of Yehuda's work has centered on the offspring of Holocaust survivors (Yehuda et al., 2001), she also saw that newborn children destined to moms who were pregnant on 9/11 had low cortisol levels, which were related to the presence of maternal PTSD. Trauma adjusts individuals' genes; henceforth, those genetic varieties could then be passed down between generations.

Jared Washington

Storytelling.

Storytelling is inseparably connected to people's historical backdrop in a bewildering assortment of oral and visual organizations. Storytelling has been a central instrument for recording individual, familial, shared, and public stories.

Aaron (2015) indicated that James (not the real name) is a clinical psychologist who works in lower Manhattan. In any case, for certain years subsequently, when a lift opened at work, he would envision individuals ablaze rushing out, their shouts filling the entryway. At any point when James shuts his eyes, he would once in a while see appendages caught in the rubble, unattended by their bodies. Snapshots of savagery and decimation tormented him that he had never witnessed. On evenings when James could not sleep, he would wander his neighborhood's roads, attempting to exorcise others' demons. In the years after the World Trade Center assaults, he treated many patients with intense and post-traumatic stress disorder. However, it took him some time to see that while his patients' psychological wellness generally improved with each passing treatment session, his own was breaking down. By 2004, he was anxious, discouraged, and incapable of sleeping most evenings; he started to undergo panic attacks for the first time in his life. Progressively, he needed to pull back from social gatherings and public spaces. He requested that a colleague prescribe tranquilizers and antidepressants.

With everyday exposure to others' trouble, an individual can develop traumatic stress disorders that imitate the PTSD of the first sources, down to the pictures of savagery that can frequent a traumatized psyche. Right now, the best medicines for trauma require sharing the story of what occurred. Talk is therapy; however, our audience can be changed for regret when the things we share are filled with horrifying experiences. This way, singular trauma can transform into something collective. Hearing accounts of outrages can likewise cause longer-term changes. These stories can change how the audience sees the world, constraining him to perceive that his friends and family may not be as safe as he had thought and confronted his helplessness to prevent future misfortunes.

This adjustment in thinking can be gradual, and it may very well be an almost oblivious cycle. At some points, you will find yourself affected by the trauma in manners you did not even expect or comprehend. You begin to see past settings that have been favorable as conceivably threatening and will find it hard to maintain your normally upbeat attitude. This way, trauma is transferred from one generation to another. Children, who are always in touch with their parents, listen to their stories of the wars, racial abuses, slavery, and likes, get to shape their own lives and future consciously or unconsciously by these same stories.

Learned Behaviors.

Trauma can likewise be passed down behaviorally. For example, trauma may unwittingly be transmitted to others through the behavior of individuals who are unable to heal from the trauma. Consequently, their children may encounter challenges with connection, separation from their more distant families and culture, and significant levels of stress from family and network individuals who are managing the effects of trauma. And this can, in turn, cause developmental issues for kids, who are especially helpless to distress at a tender age. Moreover, the offspring of somebody with post-traumatic stress disorder could learn and acquire certain parents' thinking patterns.

Many things are learned from instructors, parents, other family members, coaches, and likes. For instance, it could be discovering that we can't talk effectively to the other gender or can't converse with anyone without suffering some type of nervousness. We can learn that persons of authority are to be dreaded to the point of immediate submission; that little spaces are profoundly risky; that insects are a genuine danger; that specific foods will cause ailment; that specific body functions are irritating; that we just can't do the things that others do; that we are in some practically imperceptible way entirely different from the rest of the humankind; or any of thousands of other patterns of behavior. A portion of the things we learn can be achieved by a past trauma that we may potentially have overlooked in one way or another, even though its consequences are as yet obvious. Notwithstanding, the greater part of the things we learn happen by an ongoing, however less significant surge to the developing processes, a circumstance at times known as cumulative trauma. Any of the occasions in a chain of cumulative trauma would not be sufficiently severe to cause a problem all alone, yet taken in general, and the impacts can be significant.

Parent-Child Transmission.

There are diverse ways parents can pass down their symptoms to their children. Transmission between the parent and the child can be broken down into five measures (Harachi et al., 2006):

- Conflict.
- Communication.
- Parental involvement.
- Family Attachment.
- Parental Warmth.

Additionally, the following symptoms experienced by parents may impact their children (King-White, 2020):

1. Parents may relive traumatic events, become psychologically detached and numb, or even undergo dissociative episodes in which they become separated from

reality. These symptoms can hinder the child's ability to develop a good sense of safety and predictability in the universe.

2. Parents predisposed by trauma may be less able to react optimally during usual developmental crises and cannot help their children healthily comprehend the world.

3. Parents who have post-traumatic stress disorder (PTSD) may also have difficulty modeling a healthy sense of independence, appropriate self-soothing mechanisms and emotional regulation, and maintaining a balanced perspective when life challenges arise.

In this manner, parents refuse to separate the real suffering or agony from its setting; deportation, family members' death, companions, imprisonment, and the likes. In any case, the torment can be imparted to children and their descendants in various ways that kids pick up and fuse into their own lives without understanding what is being communicated to them. And in this manner, pass it on again in an unrecognizable structure to another generation, who at long last experience it as psychosis (the profound disorganization of mind, personality, or behavior that results from an individual's inability to tolerate the demands of his social environment whether because of the enormity of the imposed stress or because of primary inadequacy or acquired debility of his organism especially concerning the central nervous system or because of combinations of these factors and that may be manifested by disorders of perception, thinking, or affect symptoms of neurosis). The scars of the initial wound can be experienced, for instance, say a mother who has severe emotional episodes, depression, to whom the children must pay attention. They comprehend that there are pain and misery that they take on as uneasiness. Yet, they have no clue about what this is about. Their bodies experience the impacts of the transmitted agony as their distress. That can be additionally transferred to their kids, who again may not comprehend why they feel so restless. The endeavors to prevent the recurrence of the pain can likewise be experienced collectively through the manners by which a group, family, or network creates practices and methods of being together, which endeavor to hold the individuals against the danger of annihilation. The intergenerational transmission of trauma can come about due to unawareness of the impact and the stigma, which often come from the myths associated with seeking mental health support.

Understanding the transmission of Intergenerational Trauma is important when trying to grasp the concept of how it affects others. Next, we will explore the effects of Intergenerational Trauma on Black people.

CHAPTER FIVE
The Effects of Intergenerational Trauma on Black People

"Juicy"- The Notorious B.I.G.

While doing my research on Intergenerational Trauma, I had to reflect on myself. I had to ask myself how this concept that I am so passionate about affects me. I sat with this question for a while and sometimes struggled to identify certain examples. I started to think about how I was raised, what I thought about parenting, how I interacted with the opposite sex, and many other areas of my life where Intergenerational Trauma peaked its head. I realized how I cope with stress plays a part in how it affects me. I also realized how I navigated through college was a direct reflection of the impact Intergenerational Trauma had on me.

I think one interesting piece about Intergenerational Trauma's impact on myself is how I assumed you had to struggle, economically, in order for your success to be validated. I glorified and normalized what I would call "the struggle." I oftentimes found myself jealous or thinking I couldn't relate to those who I felt like didn't struggle as I did. You can guess how dangerous this form of thinking was/is. How does this relate to Intergenerational Trauma and me? I furthered this way of thinking by telling myself that my children would have to embark on this same type of "struggle" as well if they planned to succeed. Again, their success would not be valid if they didn't experience struggle. I had to check myself! I had to move past this to heal. I had to process and understand that the economic struggle isn't the only one there is. The struggle of being raised by a single parent isn't the only one there is. Some individuals are financially stable that still experience obstacles and barriers that could have hindered them from being successful. There are individuals with both parents who experience other struggles or traumas, such as domestic abuse, etc., which could have blocked their successes. Their struggle is still valid whether it looked like mines or not. Furthermore, to make sure I wasn't passing this same thought process down to my children, I had to ensure that I embraced everyone's path to success including my own and my children. Let's dive a little deeper into some other ways in which Intergenerational Trauma affects Black People.

Jared Washington

Black or African Americans – Background Information.

Population characteristics:

The African/Black American population is estimated at over 23 million people, of which the vast majority are descendants of slaves brought into the United States, U.S. However, some are voluntary immigrants from the Caribbean, Latin America, and Africa. 86% live in cities or census tracts, with over 50% or more Black/African American populations. The crime victimization rate is the highest of all ethnic groups, and other members of the same population perpetrate the majority of crime. Homicide is known to be the highest cause of death among young Black males. 35% of Black families live beneath the poverty level, 42% of the prison population is Black/African American males, 40% are in the middle economic class, and 10% of Black families are members of the upper economic class (OVC, 1998).

Historical experiences in the United States:

a. Slavery and racism: This is the unique sub-population of Americans based on migratory history. For most Black Individuals in America, their ancestors were a part of the only population that arrived on that continent as enslaved immigrants while some Whites arrived as indentured servants. There are many Native Americans taken as slaves in their land, but the effect of the importation of slaves from Africa continues to affect the culture of Black America.

b. Color has been a defining issue: African America is only a recent self-description of this specific ethnic population. Of a truth, color has been used with others to give demeaning racial labels (e.g., Redskins or Red Native Americans, and The Yellow Peril) but, African Americans alone were for centuries officially described by color (Negro; the Portuguese word for Black) while the hateful pejorative "Nigger" was the common term used among the majority population. Starting in the Civil Rights revolution in the 1960s, many African Americans replaced the Negro euphemism with Black, the descriptor they used with pride.

c. Disconnection of families: Because of slavery, the families of Black People in America were often torn apart. Children can be taken from their parents and sold off. A marriage could be torn apart at the will of the slave owner. For many Black Americans, family unification and values are a priority. To some extent, these values have been protected through matriarchy.

d. African Americans: By the end of the 1990s, many Blacks chose to call themselves African Americans as a neutral descriptor, like German Americans. As this is written, both "African American" and "Black" are considered terms of respect by the many who apply them to themselves, finally being addressed on their terms and in their terms.

Values of culture:

a. Belief in duty.

b. Time orientation is towards the future.

c. Family connections, with unique respect for mother figures, are essential.

d. Religion is a source of strength, basic Christian beliefs, but these are often supplemented by spiritualism belief.

e. Distrust of system. Other ethnicities may believe in the justice system. However, there is a traditional loss of trust in the judicial system by many Black Individuals in America due to the history of slavery in the United States.

f. Stress between the Black middle class and poor Blacks. There seems to be a distressing connection between Black Americans who have become successful and those who feel trapped in their situations of poverty and hopelessness, a reflection that the Black middle and upper classes have been developing at historical rates, but that the circumstances for the large Black underclass have been growing worse.

Culture and Trauma.

Cultural trauma is an attack on society's fabric, affecting the community's essence and its members. Trauma intersects in many various ways with culture, gender, location, history, race, and language. Cultural awareness, responsiveness, and understanding are essential to increasing access and improving care standards for traumatized families, children, and communities across the United States (NCTSN, 2020a).

Effects of Culture on Trauma.

The impacts of culture on trauma are (OVC, 1998):

i. Culture influences the perception of individuals as to the type of threat that is perceived as traumatic.

ii. Culture influences the interpretation of individuals regarding the meaning of a traumatic event. What might be a trauma under some other circumstances may comfort an individual who understands the event.

iii.Culture influences the expression of individuals and communities to traumatic reactions.

iv.Culture forms a context through which traumatized people or communities view and judge their responses. If individuals think that their society will not accept them as victims, they tend to retreat and be silent or better still, and they may accept the group's view that people with those adverse reactions are themselves to blame.

v. Culture may affect the response of the immediately traumatized.

vi. Culture may help to define healthy pathways to new lives after the trauma. The traditions and routines of the culture may help survivors of a tragedy in feeling reoriented. This reorientation is particularly true when cultures have formalized re-entry methods after a traumatic event or when cultures have a means of integrating an individual's trauma story with the culture's mythology.

Families and Trauma.

Every family experiences trauma in different ways. Some factors, such as the family's culture or ethnicity or a child's age, may affect how the family copes and regain their normal position from a traumatic occurrence. Trauma alters families as they work to survive and get used to their circumstances and environment. While this adaptation may be smooth for some, the stress and burden cause others to feel all alone, overwhelmed, and less able to maintain vital family functions. Traumas are fearful, often life-threatening, or violent events that can happen to any or all members of a family. Traumas can cause traumatic stress responses in family members with consequences that ripple through family relationships and impede optimal family functioning (NCTSN, 2020b).

Trauma and Race.

Race-based Traumatic Stress (RBTS), or Racial trauma, refers to the mental and emotional injury caused by encounters with racial bias, hate crimes, racism and discrimination directly or indirectly that is, any person that has experienced an emotionally hurtful, sudden, and uncontrollable racist encounter and abuse is at risk of suffering from a traumatic stress injury that is race-based (Helms et al., 2010; Carter et al., 2013; Villines, 2020). Media depictions of racism, such as police outrage against unarmed Black people, may also trigger racial trauma feelings. The degree of racial trauma may vary from region to region or throughout a person's lifespan (for example, racial trauma may be intensified when others deny the existence of the trauma or the victim). Unlike post-traumatic stress disorder, PTSD, it is important to note that race-based traumatic stress, RBTS, is not seen as a mental health disorder but a mental injury that can happen as the result of experiencing events of racism or living within a racist system (Carter et al., 2017).

Target Groups of Racial Trauma.

Usually, racial trauma is experienced by any marginalized or stigmatized racial or ethnic group(s); however, individuals can develop racial trauma even when they are not the victim personally.

For instance, in the United States, the U.S., Black people, Indigenous people, and People of Color (BIPOC) face racial trauma due to living under a white supremacy system. More so, Black males are also more likely than Black females to report unfair treatment by police (Villines, 2020; MHA, 2020).

Causes of Racial Trauma.

Racial trauma can be triggered by any type of stress or anxiety around racial factors or treatment. Some examples include (Villines, 2020):

i. Exposure to racial or ethnic stereotypes: An illustration of this is when textbooks or academics assert that some racial associations are better or worse at certain responsibilities.

ii. Fears about personal safety: An illustration of this scenario is when a person of Latino descent is afraid of the label of an undocumented immigrant or a person of color is scared of abuse by the cops.

iii. Witnessing members of an individual's group receiving abuse: This can be in real life or via the media, such as when a person of Latino descent sees immigrant children in shackles, or a Black person sees a video of another unarmed Black person being murdered.

iv. Racist abuse of loved ones: This cause can include attacks on spouses, children, or parents.

v. Direct exposure to racist abuse or segregation: This may be hearing racist stereotypes at work or being the racial slur recipient.

vi. Others refused to take racist experiences seriously: This may happen when people question if someone's experience was real.

vii.   Historical trauma: This is the cumulative emotional harm of an individual or generation caused by a traumatic experience or event.

viii.   Microaggressions: These are current events and are often covert in nature.

ix. Experiences of living with inequalities, such as accessibilities to schools and medical treatments.

Symptoms of Racial Trauma.

Racial trauma can affect almost every aspect of a person's well-being and wider communities (Carter et al., 2013). The indications of post-traumatic stress disorder (PTSD) are experienced by many people with racial trauma, especially after direct experiences of race-based discrimination or racist violence. Some symptoms include (Carter et al., 2017; Villines, 2020; Dove, 2020):

1. Distress relating to the trauma: This may cause a person to continually think about and relive an event. Some people have flashbacks or nightmares.

2. Avoidance: This entails things that remind the person of the trauma. It can negatively affect an individual's life in many ways. For instance, a person who experiences racism in a police interaction may fear the police or run when they see them, while a person who experiences racism at school may choose to leave the school.

3. Intensified anxiety or depression relating to the trauma: This can affect someone at any time or frequently.

4. Negative thoughts about oneself, other people, or the world at large: For instance, a person might lose trust in other individuals or worry that all authority figures want to harm them.

5. Feeling distracted by thoughts or memories of the trauma: This experience may occur from time-to-time or regularly.

6. Increased reactivity and sensitivity: A person may startle easily and become more hyper-vigilant to their surroundings.

7. In addition to the indications of PTSD, racial trauma can have other signs and symptoms, including:

8. Weathering: This is referred to as the chronic health effects of being exposed to racial discrimination and trauma. Marginalized populaces typically have worse overall health and increased risks of cardiovascular disease and other ailments. This crisis of worsened health maybe because of the lifetime of racial trauma they face.

9. Dissociation: This is the feeling of an individual being numb or disconnected from themselves or others. In some extreme cases, they might have an out-of-body experience or not remember times of dissociation.

10. Prolonged trauma and poor mental health: Unalike some other traumas, racial discrimination continuously permeate everyday life. This factor means that marginalized communities may face chronic trauma and aggression, making it difficult to recover from racist abuse.

Complex Trauma.

Complex trauma is utilized to describe children's exposure to multiple traumatic events (usually of invasive, interpersonal nature, and the wide-ranging, longing impact of this exposure. These occurrences usually begin early in life and can confuse many aspects of the child's development and the formation of a self). Black children dwelling in racially and economically segregated regions are more likely than children in other communities to experience this trauma, such as live in poverty, to be positioned in foster or substitute care, to be exposed to both familial and community outrage, to lose a loved one to violent death, to have a family member imprisoned, to experience contacts with police and the justice system, or to become homeless (Complex Trauma Treatment Network of the National Child Traumatic Stress Network, 2016).

Effects of Intergenerational Trauma on Black People in America.

Illustration

Some Black parents teach their children never to lose a receipt, to have evidence of payment in situations where they are accused of stealing. Or keeping their hands out of their pocket, so they are visible to those around them. These are just some of the many things that Black people may tell their children to keep them safe from violence linked to anti-Black racism. However, the need to constantly remind Black children about how society treats them is a traumatizing experience for a child and his or her parent. This ongoing process is referred to as intergenerational trauma, and it impacts Black communities.

African American children and families face diverse effects of intergenerational trauma (a trauma that is passed down) that they live their everyday lives trying to cope with. Some of these effects of intergenerational trauma that have been imposed on one from one generation to the next are:

The pain, hurt, fear and a sense of inferiority - these problems stem from having to live with daily harm due to racism from multiple places, including people, institutions, businesses, and lots more. This kind of trauma also turns one body into a weapon against oneself through constant reminders of one's value. Also, one is being told that one's hair is not the right texture, one's skin color is not the right skin color, and some beauty companies do not create shades that match one. Additionally, concerns that white people will see one as a threat simply by existing, or being labeled angry if one calls out racism, are also passed down.

The pressure of intergenerational trauma on Black people can lead to many health issues, from physical health to mental health. Often, there is a lack of availability within health care and Black people's wellness to seek help (Bowden, 2020).

There are mental and physical effects from these problems, including cardiovascular issues, addiction, obesity, and diabetes, along with high stress, depression, and anger (Bowden, 2020).

Despite progress and enlightenment in the United States, the legacy of slavery can be found in many areas of American society (Complex Trauma Treatment Network of the National Child Traumatic Stress Network, 2016).

Racial disparities still permeate American life, as seen with the disproportionate incarceration rates and often lethal violence directed at African Americans by law enforcement officers and civilians. More so, the direct experience of racism and race-based stressors is a strong predictor of emotional distress, psychiatric symptoms, and the development of post-traumatic stress disorder in African American children and families (Complex Trauma Treatment Network of the National Child Traumatic Stress Network, 2016).

Most of the residue of American enslavement that was culturally or race-based has formed a foundation upon which various ill effects have been embedded and possibly transferred from generation to generation with snowballing effects.

With the first generation impacted by the initial cross-cultural encounter, each successive generation is subjected to the previous generations' interface, relationship, and management of the original trauma (Barden, 2013).

The trauma that emerged out of the period has far-reaching psychological, emotional, social, and physiological legacies, which continue to plague African Americans today, manifesting in mental health issues that may also be passed on to future generations (Barden, 2013; DeGruy, 2005).

Survivor syndrome or survivor guilt, found to be prevalent in significant numbers of Jewish Holocaust survivors, can be transmitted to survivor children and other descendants (Bergmann and Jucovy, 1990).

Racism in the medical field – these results in untreated mental health issues for African American families. Examples of such cases go as follows:

Black people experience barriers when seeking mental health treatment, one of them being racism from medical practitioners. The oppressive institutions that Black people live in exacerbate their trauma. However, a more crucial one to the state of their mental health is the discrimination experienced in a medical setting. A history of racism among healthcare providers deters Black Americans from seeking treatment for mental and physical health illnesses. In the 18th and 19th centuries, Black people were easy targets when White doctors, researchers, and medical students required specimens for experiments. Their position in society during and after slavery, combined with the White belief that Black people were subhuman, made them an easy target; Black bodies' use was not to better understand physiological differences, but because they were viewed as disposable. This notion of the disposing and objectification of Black people was enforced by social norms, thus impacting Black people's mental health at that time. They were aware of what was happening to those in their community. This knowledge, combined with the general inability to do anything, deepened the wound of trauma and worsened their mental health (Savitt, 1982).

Exposure to racism, discrimination, and general race-related stress either first or second hand before or during pregnancy is an indicator of birth adversities in Black women (Rosenthal, 2011). And because of intergenerational trauma and the quality of life for Black Americans as a result of it, the stress is almost guaranteed.

In addition to Black women specifically, there is a general disregard for Black health and the disbelief of symptoms or health issues, reflecting racism among medical professionals.

The mistreatment of Black people in a medical setting is also linked to the lack of information on how illnesses affect Black bodies, especially with Black children, allowing them to go untreated or be misdiagnosed (Clarke, 2015). More so, the narrative that Black people are unruly, animalistic, or unintelligent is reinforced when Black children are met with behavioral disorder diagnoses or harsh discipline for personal misbehavior like disobedience or insubordination, thereby, exposing Black children at an early age to the effects of intergenerational trauma.

Black children are more susceptible to mental health issues because they are mostly in foster care, more frequently exposed to violence in their homes and communities, and more likely to be incarcerated, but are less likely to be diagnosed (Clarke, 2015).

Additionally, the model of how to treat mental illness does not align with Black Americans' standards. Black Americans prioritize a more personal and understanding-based approach to therapy, decreasing the power dynamic between therapist and patient (Gómez, 2015). The standard of treatment is tailored to White patients' needs, which in some ways contradict the needs of Black patients, and because of this, Black people with mental health issues are deterred from the beginning or continuing therapy.

We can talk about this problem all day long but what's the point if we don't offer solutions. Next chapter we will explore ways of healing and breaking the cycle of Intergenerational Trauma.

CHAPTER SIX
Breaking the Cycle of Intergenerational Trauma

"WIN"- Jay Rock

One thing I learned as I grew older and talked more and more about the Black experience is that we are all good, sometimes, at naming the problems but struggle with providing practical solutions. I can give you a full list of all the things that went wrong when it comes to how Black people were/are treated but very few times would I offer solutions. It wasn't until I was confronted with this by a peer that I began to think about viable solutions for our community that would help in the healing process.

In order for me to begin to think about this, I had to think about myself. I had to think about how I could heal from Intergenerational Trauma and Race-Based Trauma. I had to think about how it impacted me and how to liberate myself so that I wouldn't pass down those same trauma responses. I often say, "Let's promote a culture of healing rather than a culture of trauma." But what does that look like for me, for my family, and also my community? I figure I can give some examples I implemented before I dive deeper into some general practices.

For myself, I try to identify areas in my family history where things that I may have learned may have stemmed from trauma directly related to our experience in this country. For example, the illustration provided earlier in the book about Amadou Diallo. Another way I did this was by interviewing family members about their experiences growing up and how that impacted them and how they may have taught me lessons or messages based on those experiences. I also engage in forms of activism and support from individuals who share similar ideas and experiences as me as it related to racial traumatic events.

I try to break these cycles as it pertains to my children by identifying where the trauma lies within myself, and teach them the opposite of those trauma responses. For example, I do not touch/hit them as a form of discipline, I allow them to express their emotions as needed, and I promote self-love through daily affirmations. Let's begin to explore some more general ways of healing and breaking the cycle of Intergenerational Trauma.

Management of Traumatic Stress

There are various means to help restore an individual's emotional stability after a traumatic event. Some examples include (Cafasso, 2017):

1. Maintain a daily routine with structured activities.

2. Major life decisions, such as changing careers or moving soon after the event.

3. Give yourself time and recognize that you cannot control everything.

4. Eat a well-balanced diet, get adequate rest, exercise, and avoid alcohol and drugs.

5. Spend time with others to escape becoming withdrawn, even if you do not measure up to it.

6. Communicate the undergoing with family or close friends or in a diary or online journal.

7. Seek hobbies or other interests, but do not overstate them.

8. Request help from people who care about you or attend a local support group for people who have had a similar experience.

9. Seek a support group led by a trained professional or therapist who can facilitate discussions.

Generally, psychologists and mental health providers can work with individuals to find ways to cope with stress. They can support both children and their parents to realize how to cope with a traumatic event's emotional impact(s). More so, it is expedient that an individual seeks professional help if there is persistence in the symptoms of traumatic events and interference with daily activities, school or work performance, or personal relationships. For a child, the signs that they may need professional help to cope with a traumatic event include; emotional outbursts, aggressive behavior, withdrawal, persistent difficulty in sleeping, continued obsession with the traumatic event, and serious problems at school.

Treatment for Race-Based Traumatic Stress.

The healing tactics for an individual that is experiencing race-based trauma include (Dove, 2020; Villines, 2020):

a. Having trauma-informed psychotherapy (via a therapist who has experience working with others in the same or similar situation) helps a person identify their emotions, process their experiences, and identify healthy coping tools.

b. Finding meaning in event, context, response, and outcome. This tactic may entail engaging in social justice, spiritual, and community outlets.

c. Contextualizing one's response, that is knowing that most responses to trauma are reactions to threat.

d. Accepting support from family members and their community.

e. Receiving help from other individuals who have also experienced racial trauma.

f. Taking medication, such as antidepressants, to reduce depression or temporarily help a person sleep.

g. Learning or practicing increased flexibility in the cognitive and behavioral response to stress.

h. Making lifestyle changes, such as starting personal practices that enhance emotion-regulation and body-regulation abilities, like meditation, exercise, deep-breathing skills, muscle tension-reduction skills, journaling, and yoga.

i. Additionally, spiritual communities and practices may provide ways of making meaning, validating and sharing experiences, processing emotional and psychological responses as a group, and coordinating instrumental responses to crises.

Coping Strategies for Racial Trauma.

Finding clinicians of color or those who can identify and treat the symptoms of people with a history of racial trauma properly can pose difficult, especially for people who live in primarily white areas. Furthermore, a person might never feel cured of their trauma and continuously adopt new strategies for managing trauma. Moreover, to find the support an individual needs to manage his or her trauma can be challenging; hence, some coping skills that may help include (Villines, 2020):

i. Finding a support group that understands racial trauma.

ii. Taking part in activism against racial injustice.

iii. Avoiding relationships, when possible, with individuals who dismiss the seriousness of racial trauma.

iv. Employing self-care, including healthy nutrition and exercise, and taking some time away from traumatic experiences.

v. Going on a restricting media diet to escape images of racial abuse.

vi. Identifying racial microaggressions and role-playing how or when to respond.

vii.   Identifying racial trauma triggers and escaping them during times of increased stress.

Overcoming Complex Trauma for African American Children.

Some tips to be ensured by care providers that enhance dealing with complex trauma in African American children and families are that they can build supportive network or relationships (Complex Trauma Treatment Network of the National Child Traumatic Stress Network, 2016):

1. Getting to know the community they serve:

This is especially important for providers who do not reside in the same community as their clients. Providers need to familiarize themselves with the issues facing their clients' communities to understand children and families within their social and historical context. More so, providers should learn what it feels like; from their clients' perspective, to live in that community, what stressors and resources youth encounter daily, and what the community's racial history has been.

2. Prioritizing engagement and earning trust as essential components of treatment:

Providers, particularly those of other races or ethnic backgrounds, should understand that African American youth and families may approach services with healthy and often well-justified skepticism; hence, preparations should be made to directly address and validate expressions of distrust as appropriate and understandable, and they should also allow for ample time to learn about not only how youth and families have coped with and overcome difficulties, but also to explore positive aspects of their lives and communities and their sources of support.

3. Focusing on what youth have been through (that is, what happened to you) rather than what is wrong with them:

Schools and other systems may often view traumatized African American children and youth as having moral, intellectual, or behavioral deficits. Therefore, providers should view their services as a support to facilitate recovery from emotional and psychological injuries rather than as attempts to fix behavior or cure mental disorders.

4. Normalizing trauma reactions and provide practical tools for coping with them:

Youth, families, and children who are experiencing trauma-related symptoms are often also facing ongoing stressors in their daily lives. Therefore, providing simple ways to manage these symptoms and stressors early will free up youths' and children's internal resources for recovery and facilitate a therapeutic alliance.

5. Supporting, creating, and building upon existing positive connections:

Counteracting the effects of living in toxic systems, having connections with supportive individuals and systems is necessary.

Treatment of Intergenerational Trauma.

Treatment to tackle traumatic events is pertinent to the healing process for impacted individuals and future generations. However, mental health professionals need to describe the context and help clients understand the definitions of intergenerational trauma when seeking treatment.

Two therapeutic avenues can be used when treating intergenerational trauma. They are:

- Family therapy.

- Individual counseling.

There are various treatment methods for intergenerational trauma, all of which are usually considered from a culturally responsive perspective when availing services, including developing a safe and confident relationship with the mental health provider. Some of the modalities of therapy to take care of clients impacted by trauma are as follows (King-White, 2020):

1. Narrative Exposure Therapy (NET).

NET is a therapeutic model that emphasizes treating clients who have experienced complex or multiple traumatic experiences. This therapeutic modality also focuses on clients recounting their life events and integrates some positive events that the client has experienced. The method is usually used in group or community settings to assist clients with complex trauma challenges.

NET aims at helping clients reframe the traumatic experience in a way that allows them to contextualize the experience(s), reducing the overarching power that the traumatic experiences have had in the clients' lives. These different traumatic experiences include but are not restricted to people who have experienced political or cultural trauma (such as genocide or war in one's country or becoming refugees).

2. The Intergenerational Trauma Treatment Model (ITTM).

ITTM centers on complex trauma, especially for children and their parents and caregivers. This model is research-driven and looks at various areas related to trauma; it is informed by trauma theory, attachment theory, and advanced cognitive-behavioral techniques.

ITTM is set up to treat the unresolved trauma impact from childhood in parents and caregivers before engaging them in treatment. The parent and caregiver can involve any adult with long-term inclusion with the child. In effect, ITTM treats two generations at a time, increasing both child and parent effectiveness.

3. Trauma-Focused Cognitive Behavioral Therapy (TF-CBT).

TF-CBT is a proof-based treatment modality for children and adolescents who have signs related to trauma. This treatment method combines psycho-education and cognitive techniques to educate children and adolescents on how to express themselves, understand cognitive coping skills to deal with stressors, create and process trauma narratives, develop relaxation methods, and manage behaviors that could be detrimental to their general mental health.

Intended Treatment Outcome and Timeline.

The ultimate goal of treating traumatic experiences is to diminish the overall frequency, intensity, and severity of symptoms to not impair one's daily function. Clinicians who avail treatment for clients who have experienced trauma and intergenerational trauma indicate that the goal is not to remove memories or make life perfect; rather, treatment aims to make the indications and memories linked to the experiences bearable and manageable.

Healing from Intergenerational Trauma.

The healing process from intergenerational trauma consists of the following steps:

a) Visit one's physician: This is the very first step to healing. It is to assess any physical symptoms to ensure that what one is experiencing is not a physical or medical illness. It also aids in gaining an understanding of the triggers and symptoms of the trauma. It is noteworthy that these triggers and symptoms differ for individuals (Zaman, 2020; King-White, 2020).

b) Encourage a line of open communication with one's child: The way one models one's behavior is paramount. It is also necessary to encourage open discussion with one's child about intergenerational trauma, including cultural differences, racism, historical atrocities, and likes. (Long, 2020).

c) Family system therapy: Four strategies can be utilized during family system therapy to aid healing. They are: the use of culture-informed treatment, interruption of unhealthy family communication patterns, giving trauma a voice within the family, and helping parents offer children the permission to dissociate (Sells, 2018).

d) Seeking professional mental health support: Transgenerational trauma is effectively a form of PTSD (Post-Traumatic Stress Disorder). Finding a therapist who specializes and is experienced in treating PTSD is, therefore, necessary. It is also expedient to seek out mental health services to support one's family throughout the process. Many doctors can contact mental health providers that focus on family systems and trauma (Jacobson, 2017; King-White, 2020). The following are essential considerations when looking for a mental health professional to support one and one's family:

- Check to see if the therapist is receiving new patients.

- Ensure that they comprehend the trauma and trauma-informed practices when working with families.

- Read to ensure that the provider focuses on specialty areas specific to you and your family's needs.

- Ask if the therapist approves your insurance plan or offers affordable cash payment options.

Breaking the Cycle Associated with Intergenerational Trauma

The ability to feel safe with others is probably the most important aspect of mental health (Van der Kolk, 2015) but, it is disastrous if that which one is supposed to feel safe with (such as one's own family) are the root cause of one's source of suffering and are inhibiting one's capability of feeling safe with and trusting in others. This characteristic is the basis of intergenerational trauma. Intergenerational trauma is conducted through attachment relationships where the parent has experienced relational trauma and has significant effects upon individuals across the lifespan, including predisposition, to further trauma (Isobel et al., 2019). Fortunately, understanding this method of the transmission of trauma is now extended more widespread and given a more earnest focus than in the past (Coy, 2019).

For instance, within a society, it is very common to come across children who are victims of abuse, whose parents were also victims of abuse, who had parents that were victims of abuse, and likes. This abuse trend results in a cycle, and the cycle keeps moving (The International Society for the Study of Trauma and Dissociation, 2007).

Other forms of hostile childhood experiences that come from a variety of other mental health disorders, in addition to post-traumatic stress disorder, can be considered intergenerational trauma. Our emotional development begins from the day that we are born. Our ability to create attachments to others is also germane to feeling safe and therefore being attuned to other people. For instance, if a parent is more preoccupied with the trauma they have faced or are suffering from, they may not be emotionally consistent or stable in providing a child's proper upbringing (Coy, 2019).

It is, therefore, proven that there is an existence of an intergenerational component. The more one can work on it and stop it at its root and prevent it, the better it is for all suffering and society (The international society for the study of trauma and dissociation, 2007).

The ways that enhance breaking the cycle associated with intergenerational trauma include:

a. Educating the public to understand how their trauma (past or present) affects their families, that is, creating awareness and sensitization (Coy, 2019; King-White, 2020).

b. Availability of training to front-line professionals to help them while dealing with traumatized members of the community. For instance, if a Child Protective worker understands that when dealing with a distressed mother that has a more severely stressed baby, it is more efficient to calm the troubled mother first to have a more comforting effect on the baby, thereby, having a more active role in discontinuing the trauma (The international society for the study of trauma and dissociation, 2007).

c. Utilizing the family systems approach can also enhance dealing with and preventing intergenerational trauma. For example, the Internal Family Systems Therapy (IFS), a form of a family system's approach, focuses on self. This approach works by identifying specific self-parts to determine that they all had value and could get to work together rather than against each other. The family systems approach enables therapists to redirect and help heal pain from intergenerational trauma (Rousseau, 2019).

d. Forward movement: Moving forward in a healthy way for families is important in stopping the cycle of intergenerational trauma. Some questions to consider when moving forward throughout the process are (King-White, 2020):

• Who is a part of a person's family's support system when dealing with stressors or life changes?

• What strategies does one's family use to heal after a challenging situation?

• What does being healthy physically and emotionally mean for one's family?

• What stories or themes did one hear about one's family while growing up?

- How have these stories or themes impacted one as an individual and one's family?

Conclusion

"We as a whole convey baton we never requested yet we have not stopped to ponder, what are we conveying? Generations before perhaps have passed on the baton of scorn for the individuals who don't appear as though they like you. The political connection that you never addressed; how does this influence your locale? There's a ton of silence around what we underestimate." - Tabitha Mpamira-Kaguri

The symptoms of Post-Traumatic Stress Disorder incorporate a feeling of a foreshortened future, misrepresented startle reactions, difficulty in falling or staying asleep, upheavals of outrage, and hyper-vigilance. A portion of these practices can be found among the Black People in America today, on an individual level, yet by and large on a social level.

In the Black community, common teaching concerns a hard-working attitude: We should work twice as hard to be similar to the next individual. This way of thinking depends on social molding, anthropological attestation, and our predecessors' lived encounters. On some random day, an enslaved individual is required to work from sunup to sundown. And if they look exhausted or inefficient, they would be called sluggish or lazy and would be beaten. Many parents today do not expect that their children will get real lashes, yet the trauma from those encounters is embedded in our DNA, and on a cellular level, we review the negative results. The stress on hard-working ethic is a hyper-vigilant reaction to a centuries-old trauma and is strengthened by a longing to refute stereotypes that are circulating to this day.

Similarly, during enslavement, parents would make light of their kid's knowledge or strength to shield them from being viewed as valuable and sold on the auction block. This practice is still visible today in families where Black parents might be pleased with their kid's accomplishments and praise them at home; however, they minimize their children's gifts within sight of mixed company, so they aren't viewed as a threat. Also, do the white people believe that Black people do not feel pain, no matter how great it seems? The sentiments of dread and mistrust that so many of the Black People feel can be credited to the encounters both lived and acquired. When we consider that we are not just strolling around with our own lived encounters and injuries yet, besides those of our predecessors, we should back off and take a hard and honest look at our past. To recuperate, we should address the social trauma that has consistently been there, molding our viewpoint from birth.

Taking a look at George Floyd's final words, 'I can't breathe,' to some extent, looks like those of Eric Garner in 2014. Garner also said these words multiple times, as onlookers kept on recording his cold-blooded murder on account of cops, who nailed him down and kept on choking him, while his sobs for mercy failed to receive any notice. These words appear to reveal the lived encounters of Black People in America, whose voices have consistently been muted and characters smothered through hundreds of years of persecution and stigmatization. Racial profiling and racist equity have brought about many non-White individuals' merciless deaths for petty offenses and prompted Black men's mass incarceration, whose prospects are destroyed from the second they are placed into jail by an equity framework based on their discrimination.

Any family can be affected by intergenerational trauma. Considering the historical and racial traumatic events that have occurred, especially as relating to the Black People in America, its effects are still visible today. Therefore, if you are a Black Individual in America, this book Heal or Repeat: Breaking the Cycle of Intergenerational Trauma is for you. This way, you understand the impact of racial or historical traumatic events on you, and you can heal from this trauma and break the cycle. Be proactive, stop the cycle of intergenerational trauma, and you can get on with living a happy, secure life, and even pass on a great life to your children. You deserve it, and they also do.

REFERENCES

Aaron Reuben (2015). When PTSD Is Contagious: Therapists and other people who help victims of trauma can become traumatized themselves. Retrieved on the 2 October, 2020

https://www.google.com/amp/s/amp.theatlantic.com/amp/articl e/420282/

Administration for Children and Families (2020). Trauma. Retrieved on the 2 October, 2020 from https://www.acf.hhs.gov/trauma-toolkit/trauma-concept

Americans at Risk for Institutional Betrayal." Journal of Black Psychology, vol. 41, no. 2, SAGE Publications, pp. 121–43.

Andrew Curry, (2019). A Painful Legacy: Parents' emotional trauma may change their children's biology. Studies in mice show how Retrieved on the 2 October, 2020 from https://www.sciencemag.org/news/2019/07/parents-emotional-trauma-may-change-their-children-s-biology-studies-mice-show-how

Barden, K.P., (2013). Remembering the cultural trauma legacies of slavery: African American young adult perceptions on racism, ethnic identity, and racial socialization (Unpublished doctoral dissertation). Loyola University, Chicago, IL.

Bergmann, M.S., and Jucovy, M.E., (1990). Generations of the holocaust. New York, NY: Columbia University Press.

Bezo, B., and Maand, S., (2015). Living in "Survival Mode:" Intergenerational Transmission of Trauma from the Holodomor Genocide of 1932–1933 in Ukraine; Soc Sci Med. 2015;134:87–94.

Bowden, O., (2020). Intergenerational trauma is 'pain' passed down generations, hurting Black people's health; Global News. Retrieved on 30 September, 2020 from https://globalnews.ca/news/7085203/intergenerational-trauma-pain-Black-people-health/

Cafasso, J., (2017). Traumatic Events; Healthline. Retrieved on the 27th of September, 2020 from https://www.healthline.com/health/traumatic-events

Carter, R.T., Johnson, V.E., Roberson, K., Mazzula, S.L., Kirkinis, K., and Sant-Barket, S., (2017). Race-based traumatic stress, racial identity statuses, and psychological functioning: An exploratory investigation. Professional Psychology: Research and Practice, 48(1), 30-37.

Carter, R.T., Mazzula, S., Victoria, R., Vazquez, R., Hall, S., Smith, S., and Williams, B., (2013). Initial development of the Race-Based Traumatic Stress Symptom Scale: Assessing the emotional impact of racism. Psychological Trauma: Theory, Research, Practice, and Policy, 5(1), 1-9.

CDC, (2020) "Tuskegee Study - Timeline - CDC - NCHHSTP". Retrieved on the 1st of October, 2020 from https://www.cdc.gov/tuskegee/timeline.htm

Clarke, J.N., and Mosleh, D., (2015). "Risk and the Black American Child: Representations of Children's Mental Health Issues in Three Popular African American Magazines." Health, Risk & Society, Routledge, pp. 1–14.

Complex Trauma Treatment Network of the National Child Traumatic Stress Network. (2016). Complex trauma: In Urban African American Children, Youth, and Families. Los Angeles, CA, & Durham, NC: National Center for Child Traumatic Stress.

Coy, E., (2019). Breaking the Cycle – Intergenerational Trauma; Danielle Rousseau. Retrieved on the 23rd of September, 2020 from http://sites.bu.edu/daniellerousseau/2019/04/28/breaking-the-cycle-intergenerational-trauma/

Coyle, S., (2014). Intergenerational Trauma - Legacies of Loss; Social Work today. Volumes 14, No. 3, Paper 18. Retrieved on 23 of September, 2020 from https://www.socialworktoday.com/archive/051214p18.shtml

Davis, Angela Y., and Dylan Rodriguez. (2000) 'The Challenge of Prison Abolition: A Conversation.' *Social Justice*, 27 (3) (81), pp. 212–218.

DeGruy, J., (2005). Post traumatic slave syndrome: America's legacy of enduring injury and healing. Portland, OR: Upton Press-Joy DeGruy Publications.

Dekel, R., and Goldblatt, H., (2008). Is there Intergenerational Transmission of Trauma? The Case of Combat Veterans' children; Am J Orthopsychiatry;78(3):281.

Desilver, D., Lipka, M. and Fahmy, D. (2020.) *10 Things We Know About Race and Policing In The U.S.* [online] Pew Research Center. Retrieved on the 23rd of September, 2020 from https://www.pewresearch.org/fact-tank/2020/06/03/10-things-we-know-about-race-and-policing-in-the-u-s/

Dove, D., (2020). Racial Trauma: Origins, Signs, and Courses of Treatment; *Zencare*. Retrieved on the 27 September, 2020 from https://blog.zencare.co/racial-trauma-therapy/

Duff-Brown, Beth (2017). "The shameful legacy of Tuskegee syphilis study still impacts African American men today". Stanford Health Policy. Retrieved on the 1st of October, 2020   from https://healthpolicy.fsi.stanford.edu/news/researchers-and-students-run-pilot-project-oakland-test-whether-tuskegee-syphilis-trial-last

Duru, N. Jeremi, (2004) 'The Central Park Five, the Scottsboro Boys, and the Myth of the Bestial Black Man'. *Cardozo Law Review* 25, p. 1315.

Erdelyi K. M., (2020). Can Trauma Be Passed Down From One Generation to the Next? Retrieved on the 2 October, 2020 from https://www.psycom.net/epigenetics-trauma

Exploring your Mind, (2018). Misconceptions About Trauma. Retrieved on the 24th of September, 2020 from https://exploringyourmind.com/misconceptions-about-trauma/

Eyerrnan, R., (2004). "The Past in the Present Culture and the Transmission of Memory": Acta Sociologica. Sage Publications, Ltd. 47 (2): 160.

Fossion, P., Rejas, M.C., Servais, L., Pelc, I., Hirsch, S., (2003). "Family approach with grandchildren of Holocaust survivors": American Journal of Psychotherapy. 57 (4): 519–27.

Gómez, J.M., (2015). "Microaggressions and the Enduring Mental Health Disparity: Black

Gross, S., Possley, M. and Stephens, K., 2017. Race and Wrongful Convictions in The United States, National Registry of Exonerations, [online] Law.umich.edu. *Retrieved* on the 1st of October, 2020 from http://www.law.umich.edu/special/exoneration/Documents/Race_and_Wrongful_Convictions.pdf

Guest, (2016). Three Myths About Trauma; The Sane Blog. Retrieved on the 24th of September, 2020 from https://www.sane.org/information-stories/the-sane-blog/mythbusters/three-myths-about-trauma

Harachi, T.W., Choi, Y., Abbott, R.D., Catalano, R.F., and Bliesner, S.L., (2006). "Examining equivalence of concepts and measures in diverse samples"; Prevention Science. 7 (4): 359–68. doi: 10.1007/s11121-006-0039-0

Healing Foundation, (2020). Intergenerational Trauma. Retrieved on the 23rd of September, 2020 from https://healingfoundation.org.au/intergenerational-trauma/

Helms, J.E., Nicolas, G., and Green, C.E., (2010). Racism and ethnoviolence as trauma: Enhancing professional training. Traumatology, 16(4), 53-62.

Isobel, S., Goodyear, M., Furness, T., and Foster, K., (2019). Preventing intergenerational trauma transmission: A critical interpretive synthesis. Journal of Clinical Nursing.

Jacobson, S., (2017). What is Transgenerational Trauma?; Harley Therapy Counselling Blog. Retrieved on the 23rd of September, 2020 from https://www.harleytherapy.co.uk/counselling/what-is-transgenerational-trauma.htm

Jed Graham (2020). The Largest Mass Lynching In American History — 1919 White mobs descend on a small Arkansas community and engage in the wholesale slaughter of African Americans. *Retrieved* on the 1st of October, 2020 from https://medium.com/history-of-yesterday/the-largest-mass-lynching-in-american-history-1919-f03f5689f779

*Kent, James (1832). Commentaries on American Law **2** (2nd ed.). New-York: O. Halsted. p. 258 Retrieved* on the 1st of October, 2020 from

https://archive.org/details/bub_gb_FVoZsc_TY5IC/page/n261/mode/2up

King-White, D., (2020). Intergenerational Trauma: What It Is & How to Heal; Choosing Therapy. Retrieved on the 24th of September, 2020 from

https://www.choosingtherapy.com/intergenerational-trauma/

Legg, T.J., (2020). What is Trauma? What to Know; Medical News Today. Retrieved on the 23rd of September, 2020 from https://www.medicalnewstoday.com/articles/trauma

Long, L., (2020). A Story Of Hope: Healing From Transgenerational Trauma; One in Five Minds. Retrieved on the 23rd of September, 2020 from

https://info.1in5minds.org/blog/a-story-of-hope-healing-from-transgenerational-trauma

Mallory, Jason L. (2015) 'Denying Pell Grants to Prisoners: Race, Class, and the Philosophy of Mass Incarceration.' *International Social Science Review*, 90(1), pp. 1–27.

Mental Health America, MHA, (2020). Racial Trauma. Retrieved on 27 September, 2020 from

https://www.mhanational.org/racial-trauma

Nix Elizabeth (2019). Tuskegee Experiment: The Infamous Syphilis Study. History. *Retrieved* on the 1st of October, 2020 from https://www.history.com/news/the-infamous-40-year-tuskegee-study

Office for Victims of Crime, OVC, (1998). Cultural Perspectives on Trauma; OVC Archives. Retrieved on 27 September, 2020 from

https://www.ncjrs.gov/ovc_archives/reports/crt/chap8.htm

O'Neill, L., Fraser, T., Kitchenham, A., and McDonald, V., (2018). "Hidden Burdens: a Review of Intergenerational, Historical and Complex Trauma, Implications for Indigenous Families"; Journal of Child & Adolescent Trauma. 11 (2): 173–186.

Palwasha A., (n. d.). The Pvblication: The Trauma We Transfer Retrieved on the 2 October, 2020 from https://www.google.com/amp/s/www.thepvblication.com/amp/the-trauma-we-transfer

Raza, A. E. (2011). 'Legacies of the Racialization of Incarceration: From Convict-Lease to the Prison Industrial Complex.' *Journal of the Institute of Justice & International Studies* 11, pp. 159-170.

Reynolds John S., (1905), *Reconstruction in South Carolina*; Columbia, SC: State Co., p. 27 *Retrieved* on the 1st of October, 2020 from https://archive.org/stream/cu31924028790208#page/n37/mode/2up

Rosenthal, L., and Lobel, M., (2011)."Explaining Racial Disparities in Adverse Birth Outcomes: Unique Sources of Stress for Black American Women." Social Science and Medicine, vol. 72, no. 6, Elsevier Ltd, pp. 977–83.

Rousseau, D., (2019). Module 4 – Pathways to recovery: Understanding approaches to trauma treatment – Lesson 8.

Savitt, T.L., (1982). "The Use of Blacks for Medical Experimentation and Demonstration in the Old South." The Journal of Southern History, vol. 48, no. 3, pp. 331–348. JSTOR.

Sells, S., (2018). A family systems approach to treating intergenerational trauma. Retrieved on the 27th of September, 2020 from https://familytrauma.com/a-family-systems-approach-to-treating-intergenerational-trauma/

Small, Deborah. (2001). 'The War on Drugs Is a War on Racial Justice.' *Social Research*, 68(3), pp. 896–903.

The international society for the study of trauma and dissociation, (2007). Trauma and Dissociation in Children I: Behavioural Impacts [Video file].: Cavalcade Productions.

The National Child Traumatic Stress Network, (NCTSN), (2020a). Culture and Trauma. Retrieved on the 26 September, 2020 from https://www.nctsn.org/trauma-informed-care/culture-and-trauma

The National Child Traumatic Stress Network, (NCTSN), (2020b). Families and Trauma. Retrieved on 26 of September, 2020 from https://www.nctsn.org/trauma-informed-care/families-and-trauma

U.S. Department of Veterans Affairs (2020). PTSD: National Center for PTSD. Retrieved on the 2 October, 2020 from https://www.ptsd.va.gov/understand/common/common_adults.asp

Van der Kolk, B., (2015). The body keeps the score: brain, mind, and body in the healing of trauma. New York, NY: Penguin.

Villines, Z., (2020). What to know about racial trauma; Medical News Today. Retrieved on 27 of September, 2020 from https://www.medicalnewstoday.com/articles/racial-trauma

Villines, Z., (2020). What to know about racial trauma; Medical News Today. Retrieved on the 27th of September, 2020 from https://www.medicalnewstoday.com/articles/racial-trauma

Winter, (2012). Intervention to Address Intergenerational Trauma: Overcoming, Resisting and Preventing Structural Violence, 38pp.

Yehuda R, Halligan SL, Grossman R. Childhood trauma and risk for PTSD: relationship to intergenerational effects of trauma, parental PTSD, and cortisol excretion. Development and Psychopathology. 2001;13:733–753. doi:

10.1017/S0954579401003170.

Zaman, M., (2020). What is Intergenerational Trauma? An Expert Explains; Refinery29. Retrieved on 23 of September, 2020 from

https://www.refinery29.com/en-us/2020/06/9848448/what-is-intergenerational-trauma

Zur Institute (2014). Understanding and Treating Intergenerational Transmission of Trauma. Retrieved on the 23rd of September, 2020 from

https://www.zurinstitute.com/clinical-updates/intergenerational-trauma/

CPSIA information can be obtained
at www.ICGtesting.com
Printed in the USA
LVHW092257230721
693520LV00002B/10